CW0601474

THE CHALLENGE OF CHANGE

THE CHALLENGE OF CHANGE

Fifty Years of Business Economics

With essays by
Donald Anderson, Neil Blake,
Roger Bootle, Samuel Brittan,
Forrest Capie, R. D. Freeman,
C. A. E. Goodhart, Richard Holt,
John Kay, Jim O'Neill, David Pearce,
Colin Robinson, John Walker

Edited and with an introduction by
Jim Hirst

P
PROFILE BOOKS

society of business economists

First published in 2003 by
Profile Books Ltd
58A Hatton Garden
London EC1N 8LX
www.profilebooks.co.uk

In association with
The Society of Business Economists
International House
Queens Road
Brighton BN1 3XE
www.sbe.co.uk

Copyright © The Society of Business Economists 2003

The moral right of the authors has been asserted.
All rights reserved. Without limiting the rights under copyright reserved above, no part of this publication may be reproduced, stored or introduced into a retrieval system, or transmitted, in any form or by any means (electronic, mechanical, photocopying, recording or otherwise), without the prior written permission of both the copyright owner and the publisher of this book.

Typeset in Times by MacGuru Ltd
info@macguru.org.uk
Printed and bound in Great Britain by
Clays, Bungay, Suffolk

A CIP catalogue record for this book is available from the British Library.

ISBN 1 86197 539 2

CONTENTS

FOREWORD

In this book over a dozen distinguished economists pore over the developments in their fields over the last 50 years and try to draw conclusions for the current debate. I cannot guarantee that after reading it you will feel the issues are settled but I think you will find their contributions stimulating.

Economics is always changing, which for me is why the profession is so exciting. It is also the rationale for the existence of the Society of Business Economists, which celebrates its 50th anniversary with this volume. The SBE brings practitioners together to network, to benchmark approaches and to hear prominent speakers at its evening meetings and annual dinner and Conference. Recent speakers have included Lawrence Meyer, Mervyn King, Charles Bean, Jean-Claude Trichet, Alan Greenspan, Will Hutton, Alan Budd and DeAnne Julius. The SBE journal, *The Business Economist*, has twice won Golden Page Awards for 'readability of research'.

Numerous people have played a role in the Society's development and growth over the years, and for an account of the Society's history read Donald Anderson's excellent piece in this volume. But three people stand out for their huge contributions: Sir Campbell Fraser, who founded the group in 1953, Tadeusz Rybczynski for his twelve-year chairmanship from 1963 to 1975, during which the Society emerged more or less in the form it takes today, and Marian Marshall, who first became involved with the Society in 1968 and has been Executive Secretary since 1973. I commend them all for their efforts and dedication.

Organisations need to evolve and stay relevant if they are to survive, and the SBE has shown its resilience. With nearly 600 members and a strong calendar of meetings it is in good shape for the next 50 years. I wish it every success, and I hope readers will enjoy this book.

LORD BURNS
President of the Society of Business Economists

O ver the last 50 years the changes in geo-political configurations, economic performance, policy approaches, analytical tools and technology have been dramatic. This leaves business economists seemingly perpetually under the Chinese curse of 'interesting times'. The continuing challenge is how to make sense of economic, political and market developments in such a fast-changing world. We must try to make the best use of our training in economics and keep in touch with new academic developments, while finding answers to business questions that are, above all, practical and useful.

For this volume we have invited contributions from specialists on some of the key issues business economists have faced over the last 50 years, and indeed continue to face. Some issues are perennial, others seem to recur in cycles. Yet others are new and were unknown ten, let alone 50, years ago. Inevitably the ground covered is very broad, while at the same time far from comprehensive. But I think readers will find excellent insights into both the history of the debates in many areas and the state of play now.

Some of the authors are members of the Society of Business Economists, while others are good friends and past speakers. I would like to thank them, on behalf of the Society, for their contributions. I would also like to thank Rosemary Connell and Jill Leyland for their work in steering the book from concept to reality. Finally I would like to thank Jim Hirst for the excellent job he has done in editing this book, on top of his work as editor of *The Business Economist*.

I am sure you will enjoy reading it.

JOHN CALVERLEY

Chief Economist, American Express Bank;

Chairman of the Society of Business Economists

TABLES, CHARTS AND FIGURES

THE CHALLENGE OF CHANGE

INTRODUCTION

Jim Hirst[1]

This collection of essays was conceived as a retrospective of the work of business economists over the 50 years since they emerged as a distinctive part of the wider economics profession, and a prospective of the challenges that economists working in business may expect in applying their skills in future. It does not set out to be a comprehensive review, but reflects the particular interests of the contributors, although I have arranged the collection around three themes: the changing features of the British economy, the changing role of government with respect to the economy and business, and aspects of the contribution which economists make to the businesses that employ them. The last essay is a short history of the Society of Business Economists, whose 50th anniversary provided the impulse for the work. I commend it even to readers who are not themselves business economists. They will, I think, find in it many oblique but interesting insights into the role of the economist in business.

Of course, economists have been involved with business for as long as economics has been a distinctive branch of study. Businesses, the markets that relate them and their customers, and the wealth of the nation have after all been its principal subject matter. Academic economists have for many years been asked to advise businesses and government on matters of finance, trade, industrial activity and employment. Many more with an academic training in economics have gone into business simply to work as businessmen;

before the development of formal training in business administration, a degree in economics was widely seen as a passport to management in the larger corporations or to the civil service.

However, the emergence of economists employed in business, and in bodies such as trade associations, for their professional skills began in the aftermath of World War II. Donald Anderson, in his history, describes some of the reasons for this, but three in particular seem fundamental. First was the continuing development of macroeconomics, of theories about the relations between broad economic aggregates, such as money, spending on consumption and investment, production and employment, and of their articulation in a comprehensive set of national income and production accounts. Second was the greatly improved collection of economic statistics, in part the legacy of wartime controls. Third, and most important, was the belief, after the experience of the war and of the economic turbulence of the depressed years that preceded it, that governments should, and could, attempt to manage the economy to support employment, to hold down inflation, to improve trade, or whatever.

If changes in the economy are important to business prospects, and if economists are able to offer some insights into such changes, and into the direction of government policy, it was sensible for businesses to seek such advice in a more consistent way. As Colin Robinson remarks in the introduction to his essay on regulation, at that time business economists typically 'made economic forecasts and related company activities to them … and gave policy advice to the board'.

Central to this role of the business economist is change. It is a commonplace that the economy is constantly changing. The newspapers daily report changes in prices, in jobs, in spending, in policy. In our lifetimes we have seen profound changes in our living standards, in the industries in which we work and in the ways we buy our goods and services. The challenge to the economist is to look beneath these changes and to try to identify more enduring relationships between them which will allow him to advise businesses on the likely consequences of particular changes and on how the economy may be expected to change in future.

While this agenda is in many respects like that of any other scientific inquiry, it is clear from both John Walker's essay on forecasting and Richard Freeman's essay on business planning that business is as interested in specifically what changes to expect in the economy as in the underlying relationships. Even so, Freeman makes it clear that much of the economist's contribution to business planning has its roots in the attempt to discern trends. This may be done by deploying sophisticated techniques based on academic research, as outlined by Walker, or it may be by using simple statistical tools, informed by a knowledge of economic theory, on a few key economic data, the approach that Freeman emphasises is often used by economists directly engaged with corporate managements.

It is therefore interesting that nearly all our contributors organise the changes in the economy and in government policy over the last 50 years, and on which business economists had to advise, into several periods within each of which the economy seems to operate in a distinctive way. Of course, the greatest challenge was at the transitions, when events left some of the economist's analyses, and some economists, pointing the wrong way. It is interesting, too, how closely these periods coincide with the decades – do we see patterns in change or do we make them? Not all contributors were concerned with these periods. David Pearce, writing about sustainable business, and John Kay, writing about making business strategy, offer more continuous narratives. Their contributions point to another important role for the economist in business, and I shall return to them later.

Forrest Capie, in an opening historical overview of the period, sees a 'Golden Age' for the UK economy from 1950 to 1970, when output grew faster than ever before and unemployment was lower than ever before. It is a title which casts its glow across many of these essays, although at the time it was tarnished by the perception that other countries were doing still better. It was in any case eroded as the 1960s progressed by an inflation that spiralled out of control in the 1970s when slumps and unemployment returned. Only with the abandonment of some of the economic paradigms of the post-war consensus, in what he calls the 'triumph of the market', was inflation, slowly, brought down and output able to grow more rapidly. But unemployment never again fell below 1 per cent and output and incomes remained more volatile, until in the 1990s the growth of international trade and capital flows – 'globalisation' – seemed to offer prospects of a new golden age, until, in turn, it was blighted by the collapse of the 'dot.com' stock market boom and political uncertainties about the world economic order.

Yet, in a longer perspective, the 50 years have a unity. They were distinguished by a growth in output unparalleled in history and by inflation becoming the norm rather than the exception. In his essay Neil Blake looks more closely at some of the factors underlying the rapid growth of the golden age, the decline in the 1970s and the recovery since, while Roger Bootle's essay examines the roots of the inflation that became endemic after World War II and contributed to the end of the golden age. Both see uncertainties about whether the experience of the last half-century will continue into the next. Blake is concerned by the sustainability of output growth in the light of its effects on non-market goods – a concern echoed in David Pearce's essay on the impact of these issues on the operation of the business – and constructs a wider measure of sustainable output to illustrate this. Bootle believes that the effects of global competition and the development of anti-inflationary policy structures leave the world vulnerable to a re-emergence of the deflation that undermined the inter-war economy.

In each of these accounts we see that the changes between one period and the next are closely associated with changes in the direction of government policies. Of course, we should expect policies to change when events show them to be failing, but policies are not formed in an intellectual vacuum. They reflect the economic ideas of the time, and such intellectual paradigms are resistant to change.

Reflecting the experience of the last 50 years – and the memories of the period before that – there has been a prolonged debate over macroeconomic policies between the aims of sustaining demand and employment and of controlling inflation, and between the management of government revenues, spending and borrowing, and the management of the supply and price of money as the most effective way to achieve these aims. The essays by Charles Goodhart, Richard Holt and Jim O'Neill each examine the evolution of this argument but from three different perspectives – those of domestic monetary policy, of government fiscal policy, and of external trade and the exchange rate respectively. Of course, these are closely interwoven, and each perspective casts light on the other, but it is clear that the erosion of the so-called 'Keynesian' consensus and the emergence of the equally so-called 'monetary economics' have played a crucial role in the policies of these 50 years.[2] However, none of our authors offers any alternative to the present macroeconomic policy paradigm, and they see the only threat of a future policy regime shift in Britain's possible adoption of the euro.

Samuel Brittan's overview of the role of government in the economy also ranges across these debates, but he reminds us, first, 'how little affected by the huffing and puffing of governments' has been the underlying trend of economic growth, and, second, that government interventions have not been confined to macroeconomic management, but have also used more direct measures of planning, regulation and control, and that the work of the business economist has included the analysis of such measures which directly affect the firms and industries in which they work. Colin Robinson examines the changing nature of such intervention, moving away from government directly undertaking economic activities, and from regional and industrial policies and their associated taxes and subsidies. Robinson makes clear that these policy changes also reflect changes in the intellectual climate, and in particular the shift from a belief in 'planning' to the greater reliance on markets associated with the monetarist school of macroeconomics. However, he is not sure that Capie's 'triumph of the market' will be secure, as he sees an unresolved debate on the regulation of the operation of markets to correct where they are thought to be failing.

One class of perceived market failures that has become important over the period is those to do with the environmental and social impacts of business, and in his essay David Pearce analyses the implications for business of those concerns, and, indeed, how far they may operate through the market. These changing interventions require firms both to understand how they might be affected and to be able to debate the basis for intervention with government to ensure it does not do more damage to the effective operation of the economy than the failures it is supposed to remedy.

The growing importance of these questions in the work of the business economist has meant a renewed interest in the development and extension of the application of microeconomic analysis, with its concerns with the structures and workings of markets and industries, of prices and costs and the strategies of the firm. While Walker's essay on the changing techniques for forecasting developments in the economy addresses the macroeconomic strand of business economics which has dominated the work done in much of the past 50 years – and continues to be a common denominator in the work of economists in a wide range of organisations – Freeman, in examining the role of the economist in business planning, agrees that the analysis of trends in the economic environment, and their implications, plays an important part, but he also believes the economist can contribute to the assessment of specific product markets, of complex projects and of financial arrangements.

Still more radically, John Kay argues that the preoccupation with forecasting, an inherently erratic activity, is misconceived, and that business economists could contribute more by following their academic colleagues and focusing on issues more directly relevant to the conduct of the individual business, such as cost and pricing strategies. He believes that economic concepts provide a fruitful basis for such work. And yet, as Walker remarks, 'we all listen to the weather forecasts however much we joke about their reliability'. Business managements cannot avoid taking a view on the changing economic weather in making their decisions, and look to economists for advice.

Yet even if such macroeconomic advice continues to form a part of the work of the business economist, all our contributors agree that economies will continue to change. Deflation rather than inflation and the sustainability of economic activity rather than growth may be the issues that dominate the next 50 years, although the relation between government, business and markets seems likely to be a continuing problem. Understanding them may call for new theoretical paradigms and new analytical tools. And, if Kay is right, there is more that the economist can usefully do in the analysis of the operation of the business. The challenge for the business economist will be to develop those new tools and to change his own ways of working to contribute effectively to the businesses which look for his advice in a changing world.

Notes

1   Editor, *The Business Economist.*
2   See Chapters 6 and 7.

1

THE WORLD ECONOMY: 50 YEARS OF CHANGE

Forrest Capie [1]

Introduction

Modern economic growth, the sustained rise in the rate of economic growth, began in the eighteenth century. It began in Britain and spread through north-western Europe and North America, and ultimately around most of the world. In the nineteenth century growth was generally faster than in the eighteenth century and spread farther afield. Then growth rates accelerated again in the twentieth century to the point where no previous era had known anything comparable in the rate of expansion in, and levels of, material well-being. This has resulted in increased life expectancy, an improved living environment, and greater security. This acceleration took place very largely in the second half of the twentieth century, for the first half of the century was a period of turmoil – of war, inadequate adjustment, economic depression, and war and adjustment again.

In this paper I have simply set out the main features of this changing world economy in the second half of the twentieth century and the main indicators of its development – the background, if you will, against which business economists have had to work. The emphasis here is on the main features and trends of that 50 years. After setting the scene, I have noted the main political realignments that took place and how they affected the changes in the economy. This is followed by some brief consideration of what was a major turning point in the 1970s, of the triumph of the market that followed and of the globalisation that has characterised the closing years of the century.

Setting the scene

Some brief comments need to be made first about the background to the remarkable growth in the second half of the twentieth century. The late nineteenth century was also a period of considerable economic development and of increasing economic integration, or what we would now call globalisation. Following the American Civil War in the 1860s and the revolution in transport and communications that took place in the 1870s in rail and shipping, and with the coming of the telegraph in the 1860s, economic development spread rapidly around the world. The doctrine and practice of free trade, both of which were pursued and exported by Britain, were at a high point, until late in the period, and more countries were drawn into the world economy as trade grew rapidly. Primary products flowed from the farthest reaches of the world to the European markets, and capital goods and manufactures flowed out in return. Capital flowed to these countries too on an ever-increasing scale – indeed, on a scale comparable to that of the late twentieth century. A strong international monetary system in the form of the gold standard prevailed. By some measures the world economy was even more integrated in the 1890s than it was in the 1990s. But at the same time there was an emerging reaction against this globalisation, and nationalism, together with its economic manifestation protectionism, began to spread. Indeed, this reaction carries much of the blame for the collapse into war and depression that followed.

The developing world economy of the late nineteenth century came to an abrupt halt with the outbreak of World War I in 1914. Trade, capital flows, migration and the international monetary system were all seriously disrupted. The war was not without its economic advantages in terms of technological advance, and even in the fields of management and production there were striking improvements. But the costs – beyond the human suffering and loss of life – were enormous. All manner of problems were born, most of which were not to be resolved properly in the decade after the war. Some of them played a part in the coming of the depression that was so devastating for much of the world at the end of the 1920s. Apart from the disruption to trading patterns, huge war debts accumulated and massive reparation payments were imposed on Germany. Hyperinflation and exchange-rate misalignment contributed to the distortions. The great depression followed in 1929–32 and beyond, and so severely damaged growth around the world that recovery was not achieved until the end of the 1930s. By that time another war had become inevitable.

An important legacy of the two world wars and the inter-war depression was the view that governments could do better than markets. Indeed, the idea that markets failed became widespread, and the obvious response at the time was that governments should intervene in, or more commonly substitute for, the market. Throughout World War II discussions were held among the allies, though often this meant between the USA and the UK, on the shape of the world economy after the war. The principal objectives were to escape from the problems and the solutions of the 1930s – trade protection, currency devaluation, self-sufficiency, and so on. Some good came out of this in the form of the International Monetary Fund and the General Agreement on Tariffs and Trade. These laid down the basis for a stable international monetary system and led to the increasing relaxation of restrictions on trade. On the domestic front there were, however, retrograde steps. The prevailing interpretation of the events of the 1930s was that markets had failed and governments had to replace them. This resulted in the widespread nationalisation of major industries and other forms of intervention.

However, the most immediate threat in the 1940s was that from communism and the looming ambitions of the Soviet Union.

The rapid recovery of western Europe was seen as one means of containing that threat. Hence there was a desire to ensure that recovery and the Marshall Plan was at the centre of this as the USA made huge loans and grants to the European countries.

There are seldom any clean breaks in history and 1950 is not one either. But much of the post-war adjustment had taken place by then, although the Korean War was about to break out. Nevertheless, it was from this juncture that much of the world began to embark on a period of most striking economic progress.

Growth of the world economy

The world economy grew at a remarkable pace through the second half of the twentieth century, though there were interruptions along the way. The period from 1950 to 1970 is widely referred to as a 'Golden Age'. Many OECD[2] countries experienced dramatic improvements in their economic fortunes in these years. However, the 'world economy' was a much smaller one in 1950 in several respects. There were fewer countries and a much smaller total population. The Soviet Union and its satellites in eastern Europe largely excluded themselves from the rest of the world economy. And communist China, too, was essentially closed.

Nevertheless, between 1950 and the end of the century the world GDP[3] grew from 5.3 billion 1990-value dollars to over 33.7 billion. Growth was fastest of all in Asia, where output rose by a factor of 12. In western Europe it grew fivefold. Even Africa grew fivefold. To see what that meant for living standards we need to take account of population growth. And although population more than doubled, from 2.5 billion to almost 6 billion, the growth of income was vastly greater. This was obviously true in western Europe, where population grew by less than a third, but was also true even in Africa and Latin America, where population trebled in size.[4]

The period of greatest growth was that from 1950 to the beginning of the 1970s. For example, real GDP per head in Europe grew at 3.8 per cent per annum in these years, more than twice as fast as any comparable previous period and more than twice as fast as the following twenty years. Economic growth in Japan was even faster. Many explanations have been offered for such a performance. US aid was important in the early stages of recovery in Europe, although it varied greatly across countries. In the case of Japan and some others there was undoubtedly technological catch-up. The improving international environment of freer trade played its part, as did the desperate need to restore capital equipment and raise consumption following a long period of neglect.

World trade grew even faster than output. For example, world exports measured in 1990-value dollars grew from nearly 300 million in 1950 to almost 6 billion by the end of the century, that is by a factor of 20. In this Golden Age German exports were growing at an annual rate of over 12 per cent, America's by over 6 per cent, and Japan's by more than 15 per cent. For the world as a whole the figure was 8 per cent All these growth rates slowed in the following quarter-century to 4.4, 6.0, 5.3 and 5.1 respectively, but this was from a higher base, and still represented considerable growth.

The explosion in capital flows came later. They were constrained under the Bretton Woods arrangements[5] but when freed grew rapidly, reaching their greatest rates in the 1990s. It is not easy to be precise about the scale of capital flows. Distinguishing net and gross is just one problem. But there can be little argument about the huge scale. One indicator is that foreign exchange trading in the 1970s was of the order of 10 to 20 billion dollars. By the mid-1990s it was around 1,260 billion dollars – close to 100 times greater.

Major political realignments

In the Western world at the outset of these 50 years there were two political developments which were important for the world economy. One was the end of empires and the other was the formation of the European Community that would in time become the European Union.

A principal feature of the post-war world was the retreat from empire. European countries that had colonised the world in the late nineteenth century came under pressure to return sovereignty to what had been colonies. Some former dependencies simply declared independence. Since the war had been fought in terms of freedom and democracy this was both to be expected and was not seriously resisted. Some of the transfers were successful and some less so. The British experience was on the whole successful, although there were many setbacks in the process. By 1965 all British colonies in Africa were independent except Southern Rhodesia. The French experience in Algeria and the Belgian experience in the Congo were much more difficult. Countries that gained their independence did not immediately blossom, for they were often not well equipped to direct their own affairs; in fact they almost invariably regressed. The colonial powers had not prepared the way for the transference of power – indeed, in many cases they could not, given the pressing demands that were being made. Although suitable legal systems were frequently in place, education was not advanced and there was often disagreement among the different domestic political parties, disagreement that too often ended in civil war, with the inevitable human and economic costs.

The second important feature was the emergence of the beginnings of the European Union. Almost as soon as the war was over schemes were devised and implemented to bring the countries of Europe together. This was motivated partly by politics and partly by economics. The former motivation was directed at preventing future war in Europe. There was also the desire on the part of some to offer competition to the USA and the Soviet Union, which otherwise looked like being superpowers set to dominate the world. On the economic front there were schemes for cooperation and the integration of some industries (coal and steel, for example). In 1957 the Treaty of Rome created the European Economic Community or Common Market. This marked the beginning of the process that would lead to ever greater cooperation and integration. A scheme for monetary union was also launched and was finally achieved for most of the Union in 2002. Many saw this as essentially politically motivated, for a monetary union really requires a fiscal union to support it and this in turn requires increased centralisation of political power.

The turning point

The end of the Golden Age came with the accelerating inflation of the late 1960s. Thus was in large part a consequence of the financing of the Vietnam War and of large government expenditures on the 'great society'. The fixed exchange-rate regime then transmitted the inflation around the system. The USA had to finance what was an unpopular war by money creation rather than by more conventional taxing and borrowing. The result was inflation, first in the USA and then around the world with the inflationary pressures transmitted through the exchange-rate system. This was becoming clear towards the end of the 1960s and led inevitably to the breakdown of the international monetary system at the beginning of the 1970s. The world at that point moved to an entirely fiat monetary system for the first time in history, ensuring that inflation would persist for much longer – in fact until people tired of it and governments were obliged to take action to curb it.

Inflation was one of the striking features of the world economy in the second half of the twentieth century. Remarkably, most market economies in this period experienced at least one episode when inflation exceeded 25 per cent. Many contended with inflation of more than 100 per cent that lasted for some years. In the 'transition' economies the experience was far worse. Most of them experienced inflation of more than 400 per cent at some point in their transition. All this had a damaging impact on economic performance. So the great achievements that were made could have been even greater.

Further, at the end of the Golden Age there was a downturn in many economies; but there was a good deal of misinterpretation of this change in the real economy and how recovery might be effected. The response to the recession at the beginning of the 1970s was generally to turn to expansionary policies of a 'Keynesian'[6] kind. Under floating exchange-rate regimes expansionary monetary policies could be used, it was believed, to boost incomes. But of course, as some leading economists had been pointing out for some time, these policies would produce inflation in the long run without any benefit to output. And inflation is what followed.

There were at least two contributory factors involved. One was trade union power. It was widely believed that powerful unions were pushing up wages and producing 'cost-push' inflation. It is clearer now that weak governments were giving in to union pressure and printing the money required to settle large wage demands. The second factor was oil-price rises brought about by the oil producers' cartel. The first of these came in 1973 and the second significant one in 1978. Again the price of one item rising does not produce let alone cause inflation, even if that item is a large one in the economy. What happened, and with some justification in order to ease adjustment, was that governments again printed money to accommodate the increase in prices. These monetary expansions certainly contributed to the increasing inflation around the world. Inflation in several OECD countries reached annual rates of around 20 per cent.

But the real economy did not improve. Instead it languished in the doldrums, and this gave birth to the new term 'stagflation' – stagnant output with inflation. This was the point at which, at least in some countries, there was a growing realisation and acceptance of the fact that there needed to be more attention to the supply side of the economy, with changes to its structure and working. The real economy had become over-regulated and taxed, lacking the appropriate incentives to produce at its most efficient. Thus it was that in the recession in Britain at the end of the 1970s policies were adopted which looked to many to be tightening rather than expansionary and were widely condemned as such. But in fact they signalled the beginning of supply-side changes that were to arrest the relative decline of the British economy.

Triumph of the market

The last twenty years or so of the twentieth century could be labelled the 'triumph of the market'. It was at this time that there was increasing recognition that while there may have been less than ideal market outcomes, so there were less than ideal government outcomes. In its crudest form this could be seen from casual inspection of the two great competing systems – those of the centrally planned economies and those of the market – or, more accurately, mixed – economies. But even within these mixed economies it was becoming clear that less intervention produced better results. Thus it was that around the world all kinds of markets began to be deregulated, labour markets freed, barriers to trade reduced, capital markets liberalised, and so on.

The growing divergence between the economic performance of the market economies and the centrally planned economies undoubtedly contributed to the demise of the latter. At the end of the 1980s, following growing pressures, the countries of eastern Europe began to overturn their largely Soviet-imposed communist regimes and opted for market economies. Within the Soviet Union there were similar pressures which initially were addressed by means of reform – 'perestroika'. But in the end a complete overthrow of the old system was necessary and was realised. None of these transitions from one regime to another was easy, primarily because the fundamental requirements of a market economy, well-defined and enforceable property rights, were absent. But at the turn of the millennium most of them seemed to be on a sustainable course.

Globalisation

In the last decade of the twentieth century the watchword that was increasingly heard was 'globalisation'. A new world order seemed to be developing with more and more countries intimately bound up in the international institutions and with other countries. Trade and capital flows were growing faster than ever, and following the collapse of the Soviet empire more countries were drawn into the world economy. China too began to be more open.

Another feature was that a large number of less-developed countries that had been pursuing protectionist and interventionist policies (misguidedly advocated by many development economists of the time) began to reverse these policies. Liberalisation became the fashion. Deregulation of all aspects of economies was pursued. Sometimes the sequencing of these policies was not ideal and led to frustration and less than desirable outcomes. But lessons were learned and there was dramatic growth in many parts of the world as such countries made much progress. Much of Latin America could be included in this group. Many of the countries of East Asia acquired the label 'tigers' on account of their extremely rapid growth and aggressive pursuit of material success. And countries such as India and China, which had both been sluggish economic performers over a very long period, also began to grow rapidly. Trade and capital linkages were extended further and further and the world economy became increasingly integrated.

Just as there had been in the late nineteenth century, so now there were many reactions against this globalisation. Some of these were given a fillip when the countries of East Asia experienced crises at the end of the 1990s. Japan was at the heart of this. It had been a major source of capital to the emerging economies of that area, but the growth of its economy had been slowing down in the course of the 1990s, for a number of reasons. When Japan, as a consequence of its own banking difficulties, needed to repatriate capital from those countries, problems developed and were exacerbated by the withdrawal of other capital and subsequent exchange-rate difficulties. Much of this was seen by some as the inevitable consequence of globalisation and the supposed destabilising effects of capital flows. However, there were deeper problems in most of these countries which had to do with their weak banking systems, lax monetary and fiscal policies, and the moral hazard created by governments fostering the idea that important companies would not be allowed to fail.

Another notable feature of the twentieth century was the growth of big business and the spread of the multinational corporation. Both have been around for a long time, but the vast increase in their number was a twentieth-century phenomenon. And again it was in the Golden Age that the fastest growth in the number of large firms took place. For example, to give some European cases, the number of firms employing more than 10,000 people rose in Britain from 65 in 1953 to 160 in 1972, in France from 20 to 62, and in Germany from 26 to 102. Thereafter growth steadied, possibly because the expected economies of large-scale operation never materialised, so that there was little change in these numbers by the 1990s. But as the world has become increasingly integrated, it is not surprising to find such companies spreading their activities around the world and the number of multinationals increasing.

Looking ahead

In the 1970s it became fashionable to talk of the end of economic growth, or at least to think in terms of the costs of growth and consider the potential limits to growth in the light of these costs. By the 1990s that had all disappeared. Talk was then of the 'new economy' and the possibility that economic growth was about to become faster than ever before. The information technology revolution lay behind the idea that perhaps productivity could be – indeed in some countries already seemed to be – raised to new levels, and that the trend rate of growth of output would be raised in countries most receptive to the revolution. At the time of writing there is insufficient evidence to reach conclusions on this. Many of the signs are promising, but there are also some cautions. In an echo of the debates of the 1970s, there are widely voiced concerns over the impact of economic growth on the environment and calls for government intervention, even if in most cases a more sensible solution would be a better allocation of property rights. And domestic regulation, whose spread is difficult to resist, can still damage otherwise promising possibilities.

Notes

1   Professor of Economic History at the City University Business School, London.

2   Organisation for Economic Cooperation and Development, established in 1961 and comprising by 1964 21 industrialised countries, including the USA, Japan, Canada and most countries of western Europe.

3   GDP stands for Gross Domestic Product. It is the most commonly used measure of the total output of goods and services in the economy of a country, based on a system of national income and expenditure accounts. It is 'domestic' in that it excludes goods and services produced outside the country by its nationals, and 'gross' in that it does not allow for any depreciation of capital stocks. It can be measured in the prices current each year, or in the constant prics of a base year. Changes from year to year when measured in constant prices are often referred to as 'real' or 'volume' changes.

4   Angus Maddison, *The World Economy: A Millennial Perspective*, OECD, Paris, 2001.

5   The international monetary arrangements for the post-war world devised in 1944 at Bretton Woods in New Hampshire, USA. In fact these were considerably modified before actually being implemented.

6   Policies emphasising the management of total spending in an economy primarily through government borrowing, spending and taxation, and deriving, at some remove, from ideas advanced by John Maynard Keynes. See Chapter 7 – *Ed.*

2

ECONOMIC GROWTH IN THE UK

Neil Blake [1]

Introduction

Over the 50 years to 2001, the output of the UK economy (measured by GDP at constant, 1995, prices) has increased by 343 per cent. This is equivalent to an increase of 288 per cent per person. These are the fastest growth rates ever recorded by the UK over such a lengthy period. Despite this achievement, the UK's record on economic growth has not all been plain sailing. Growth has been uneven, and over the period we have seen the economy go from full employment to mass unemployment and back to low unemployment. Comparisons with other major international economies over the whole period are very unfavourable, although the UK has performed better over more recent years. Further, there is even a debate about whether or not GDP is the appropriate measure to use.

The first section of this chapter looks at how economic growth has varied over the 50-year period and offers some thoughts on why growth rates have varied. The second section puts this into an international context, looking at both comparative economic statistics and reviewing some of the ideas about why international growth rates differ. The third section considers how appropriate GDP is as a measure of growth and looks at the results using alternative measures that bring environmental degradation and resource depletion into the equation. The fourth section concludes

---

Figure 1 **Real GDP growth in the UK, 1951–2001**

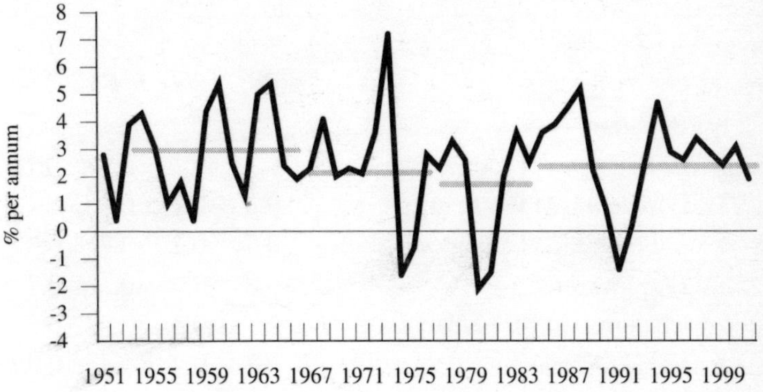

Source: National Statistics.

---

by offering some tentative thoughts about what the next 50 years might have to offer.

Economic growth in the UK over the last 50 years

As Figure 1 shows, the pattern of economic growth over the past 50 years has been far from smooth (nor indeed was it so in previous decades). The 1950s and 1960s were punctuated by stop-go policies whereby expansionary policies were inevitably reined in by inflation, balance of payments and exchange-rate problems. The final fling of this era was the Barber Boom of 1972–3, which was eventually punctured, first by problems of rising inflation and then by the impact of the first OPEC[2] oil-price hike. The result was the first year-on-year contraction of GDP in the post-war era.

A combination of the second oil-price shock in 1979 and the monetarist experiment[3] ushered in the second post-war recession in 1981–2. This was followed by a sustained upturn, which eventually culminated in another inflationary bubble that burst, leading to the third post-war recession in 1991. Since then, the UK

Table 1 **Accounting for UK economic growth, 1953–2001 (per cent per annum)**

		1953 –67	1967 –77	1977 –85	1985 –2001
1	Population	0.6	0.2	0.1	0.4
2	Changing dependency rate	-0.3	-0.1	0.5	0.1
3	Population of working age	0.3	0.1	0.6	0.4
4	Labour market changes	0.5	-0.2	-0.7	0.3
5	Employment	0.8	0.0	-0.1	0.7
6	Changing full-time/part-time mix	-0.1	-0.1	-0.3	-0.2
7	FTE employment	0.7	-0.2	-0.4	0.6
8	Productivity	2.2	2.6	2.2	2.0
9	GDP	2.9	2.4	1.7	2.6
10	GDP/head	2.3	2.2	1.6	2.2

Source: National Statistics; author's calculations.

economy has enjoyed the longest period of stable growth of the entire 50-year period.

Short-term fluctuations often obscure changes in the underlying performance of the economy. As well as showing year-to-year changes, Figure 1 (and Table 1 above) also identifies four distinct periods of growth.[4] These indicate an underlying growth rate for GDP of 2.9 per cent per annum between 1953 and 1967 (or what has been termed the 'Golden Age' of UK economic growth). This fell to 2.4 per cent per annum between 1967 and 1977 and then fell again between 1977 and 1985. The final period, 1985–2001, saw a return to much higher growth rates, the highest since the Golden Age.

Having identified distinct periods of underlying economic growth, we can go a stage further and ask the more interesting question: what factors accounted for the observed changes? Table 1 is an exercise in growth accounting that focuses on the impact of changes in demographics, in labour markets and in productivity, and in what follows these are examined in greater detail to suggest some answers to that question.

Demographics are a key determinant of labour supply, along with secular trends in participation. Table 1 shows how changing rates of population growth and changes in the age structure of the population interacted to produce the observed change in the population of working age. Although the Golden Age was the period of the most rapid increase in population, much of this was associated with the post-war baby boom, and the working-age population did not grow particularly rapidly. In 1967–77 working-age population growth almost ground to a halt. Baby-boomers made their major impact on labour supply between 1977 and 1985, and this effect has continued to a lesser extent into the most recent period.

Changes in working-age population, however, do not always bring about corresponding increases in employment. We have termed the difference between employment and working-age population growth 'labour market changes'. This comprises two distinct parts. First, it picks up non-demographic labour supply-side changes, such as increases in female participation or changes in the discouraged-worker effect.[5] An increase in female participation was the big reason for the positive contribution of labour market changes in the Golden Age. Second, this measure also picks up changes in the efficiency of the labour market, or shifts in the non-accelerating inflation rate of unemployment (NAIRU). The big negative labour market changes came in the 'stagflation' of the 1970s and 1980s, when claimant-count unemployment jumped from around 4 per cent to more than 10 per cent of the workforce. This period saw the biggest increase in working-age population while recording the worst employment record.

The abysmal labour market performance of the middle two periods was the result of long-standing flaws in the supply side of the UK economy being exposed by successive oil-price shocks and the subsequent rise in inflation (though the build-up of inflation actually preceded the first oil-price shock). These related to difficulties with industrial relations, inflationary pay pressure and restrictive practices by trade unions, poor management (partly associated with the weakness of the link between ownership and management) and a lack of competitive pressures, particularly in the public sector.[6] The sharp impact of high energy prices, increased competition from newly industrialised countries on manufacturing industry, and the time taken for the economy to adjust to being more service oriented did not help. An industrial policy focused on manufacturing, and with a tendency to support lame ducks, did not smooth the transition.

In the final period there was a distinct improvement in labour market conditions, which has contributed an average of 0.3 per cent per annum to economic growth. This has happened despite a levelling off in female participation, big increases in early retirement and increased participation in higher education. The main reasons for the improvement have, in turn, been improvements in macroeconomic conditions[7] and, especially, in the flexibility of labour and product markets. This in turn was associated with the supply-side reforms initiated by Mrs Thatcher's first government[8] and pursued by all subsequent governments, including the current one. While these policies have had their downsides, particularly in terms of job losses, diminished job security and increased inequality (see the third section), they have undoubtedly made a major contribution to the UK economy's ability to create jobs and to adjust to macroeconomic shocks.

The effects of changes in employment on labour inputs to the economy must also allow for the changing mix of full- and part-time employment. We could be a little more sophisticated and look at changes in actual hours worked, but consistent data over such a long period are problematic, and in any case the change in the full-time/part-time mix captures the bulk of the fall in average hours worked.

The final contribution to growth comes from productivity improvements (defined here as GDP per full-time equivalent person employed). Productivity growth has not been a strong point of the UK economy over the last 50 years. It was not particularly strong in the Golden Age and has actually been weakest in the most recent period, even though output growth has been quite respectable. The reasons for poor productivity growth are similar to those given for poor labour market performance in the past, together with the related weakness of investment (generally and in research and development in particular), to which we might add the flaws in the UK education and training system.

It might be a little surprising, therefore, that productivity growth has actually weakened in the most recent period, despite the supply-side reforms that we have credited with much of the improvement in the labour market. There are a number of reasons why recent productivity growth has disappointed. First, the rapid increase in employment, particularly since 1993, has led to what is sometimes known as the 'batting average effect'. This means that, as employment rises, more marginal and less productive workers are taken on, and this has the impact of decreasing average rates of productivity. Second, rapid employment growth has also been associated with a number of less well-paid occupations in the retail, restaurant and personal care areas (as well as the boom in information and communication technology – ICT – and other professional jobs).[9] Third, there has been a continued run-down of manufacturing's share of both output and employment which, given that manufacturing has above average levels of productivity, has tended to drag down aggregate productivity – although the advent of North Sea oil and the telecommunications boom should have tended to raise average productivity. Fourth, although privatisation has helped to promote competition and efficiency in many cases, it has clearly worked less well in others, especially when the problem of regulating a natural monopoly is particularly difficult. Finally, many of the policies that have been put in place to address the UK's problems with education and skills have either not worked or have not had time to work or to filter through to the workforce.

To sum up, we have identified four distinct periods of economic growth that span the last 50 years. The overall picture is one of a gradual slowing in the underlying rate of GDP growth until 1985, since when there has been a marked acceleration.[10] The main reason for the slowdown was a combination of labour market factors. An improvement in the labour market appears to be responsible for all of the improvement in the period since 1985 as productivity growth has continued to disappoint.

International comparisons

The consensus view has been that the post-war history of the UK economy was one of relative decline, which was halted, but not reversed, by supply-side policies introduced from 1979 onwards.[11] Tables 2–4 show some comparative international growth statistics which tell a rather more positive story.[12] Table 2, which for consistency uses the same benchmark years as Table 1,[13] shows the relative decline clearly enough, with the UK having the slowest GDP growth of the countries shown in each of the first three sub-periods. Where the data differ from previous estimates is for the final period, 1985–2001, where the latest data actually show the UK to have been the second fastest-growing of the world's large economies.

In terms of GDP per head, the UK was actually the fastest-growing economy. The consequences of the UK economy's renewed vigour over the past fifteen years show up dramatically in the GDP per head comparisons in Table 4. Having had the lowest level of GDP per head (for the six major economies compared) in 1985, by 2001 the UK had advanced to third place, ahead of each of the other large European economies and with a narrower gap with both the USA and Japan.

There are two main reasons why we can now claim that the UK economy has started to overtake or to narrow the gap with other large economies when the estimates published by Crafts could claim only very modest relative progress.[14] One is that we can now compare the growth performance to 2001 whereas Crafts only looked at the period to 1996. The other is that we have been able

Table 2 **GDP growth: international comparisons**
         (per cent per annum)

	1953–67	1967–77	1977–85	1985–2001	1953–2001
UK	2.9	2.4	1.7	2.6	2.5
USA	3.8	3.2	3.0	3.0	3.3
Germany	5.5	3.6	1.8	1.7	3.2
France	5.2	4.2	1.9	2.3	3.5
Italy	5.7	3.9	2.6	2.0	3.6
Japan	9.0	6.5	3.8	2.4	5.4

Table 3 **GDP per head growth: international comparisons**
         (per cent per annum)

	1953–67	1967–77	1977–85	1985–2001	1953–2001
UK	2.3	2.2	1.6	2.2	2.1
USA	2.2	2.1	2.0	1.9	2.0
Germany	4.8	3.4	1.9	1.3	2.8
France	4.1	3.5	1.4	1.8	2.7
Italy	5.0	3.3	2.3	1.8	3.1
Japan	7.9	5.3	3.1	2.1	4.6

Source: see note 12.

to make use of more up-to-date estimates of relative GDP levels which incorporate both the latest data on the new system of economic accounts[15] and the latest estimates of cross-country price differences. Note also that the figures presented here for Germany are for the whole of Germany while the data in Crafts were for West Germany only.

Leaving the details of the data aside, the general messages of Tables 2–4 are clear. The first sub-period, 1953–67, may have been the Golden Age of UK economic growth but it was also the period of the most rapid relative economic decline. Relative decline continued, albeit at a lesser rate, between 1967 and 1977.

Table 4 **GDP per head (2000 PPS, UK = 100)**

	1953	1967	1977	1985	2001
USA	149	146	145	149	141
Germany	72	101	113	115	99
France	73	93	105	103	96
Italy	61	89	99	104	97
Japan	34	72	96	108	105

Source: see note 12.

The disruptions to the international economy of the 1970s affected all the major economies but the UK remained the slowest. From 1985, the UK has advanced up the growth league and actually out-performed the USA in terms of growth in GDP per person.

The obvious reason for the UK's relative economic renais-sance (at least as measured by GDP growth) is the impact of supply-side reforms. Employment rates are much higher in the UK than in most other European economies, and although pro-ductivity levels still lag behind this may be linked to the 'batting average effect'. Looking at relative GDP per head growth over the period from the 1970s to the 1990s, Bassanini and Scarpetta[16] found that an improvement in human capital, demographics and the exposure to international trade all benefited the UK relative to the OECD average, while it had been disadvantaged by a low investment share in GDP and other unidentified effects. The UK's investment share is now on a par with most other countries, and supply-side reforms have probably eliminated much of Bassanini and Scarpetta's unexplained effects, leaving the UK in a rather stronger relative position.

Alternative measures of economic well-being

The discussion in the first two sections has focused on GDP or GDP per head as a measure of economic progress. GDP is a measure of market economic activity.[17] It measures the market value of economic activity carried out within certain geographical boundaries. It is not a suitable measure of the resources available to the population of that area, as it includes the value of output remitted abroad as the interest profits and dividends received by foreign companies and citizens. Alternative measures that take this into account and look at the actual purchasing power generated by economic activity are available (e.g. national disposable income). For the UK and other large economies, these tend not to be too different from GDP, but for smaller economies the differences are sometimes quite large.

More seriously for the UK, GDP is a gross measure that does not take into account the impact of economic activity on things such as the environment or the quality of life. Weitzman,[18] for example, estimates that if we were to take account of the costs of mineral depletion in measuring GDP, it would reduce estimated growth rates by 1 per cent. There have also been more comprehensive attempts at holistic estimates of economic output, beginning with the USA[19] and subsequently extended to a number of other countries.[20] These estimates start off with national accounts estimates and then try to adjust them to produce an estimate of the change in 'sustainable economic welfare' rather than just market economic activity. The Index of Sustainable Economic Welfare (ISEW)[21] for the UK takes consumer spending and government consumption (including spending on health and education) rather than GDP as a starting point. This is then adjusted to take account of four main factors: income inequality, non-market production, net private and public investment, 'defensive' expenditure (see below) and the costs of resource depletion and environmental degradation.

The argument for making adjustments for inequality is that the utility received by consumption declines the higher the level of consumption of the individual (i.e. that there is a declining marginal utility of consumption). This, it is argued, means that the market value of consumption should be adjusted to reflect the level of and changes in inequality. In the case of the UK, the adjustment for inequality has the effect of reducing the value of consumer spending, as estimated for the National Accounts, by only 6.6 per cent in 1977 but by up to 14.3 per cent in 1996. This is the equivalent of reducing growth by about half a per cent a year.

GDP measures only market activity, so it seems appropriate to add on some allowance for the value of non-market activities, such as work done in the home. This does, however, raise problems of measurement. National Statistics have recently produced a comprehensive set of household accounts, but historical evidence on a consistent basis is harder to come by. Jackson et al. use a variety of historical time-use surveys to put their series together. Surprisingly, they find little change in the amount of non-market work done over the past 50 years. The estimated value of the work, however, increased nearly threefold between 1950 and 1996 because they use average domestic wages as a way of valuing time spent. This increase is recorded even though they do not include time spent driving as a useful activity – although this seems a little odd, as driving time is a direct substitute for public transport, which is measured in consumer spending. On the whole, although there is a good theoretical case for trying to value non-market activity, uncertainty over historical estimates means that we need to be cautious about giving too much weight to the estimates of changes over time.

The addition of net investment moves the measure a little closer to GDP, which includes gross investment. Net investment is more appropriate in that it excludes the value of capital equipment used up by the production process. 'Defensive' spending is that which does not add any extra benefit to consumers but which is undertaken just to maintain the present situation, and is therefore excluded from the index. Examples include defence spending by government and the cost of cleaning up environmental damage, as well as what are deemed non-beneficial travel costs such as commuting costs. The argument could probably be taken even farther

Table 5 **The Index of Sustainable Economic Welfare
compared with GDP (per cent per annum)**

	1953–67	1967–77	1977–85	1985–96	1953–96
GDP	2.9	2.4	1.7	2.5	2.5
ISEW	2.4	3.0	-1.5	-0.9	0.9
GDP/head	2.3	2.2	1.6	2.2	2.1
ISEW/head	1.8	2.8	-1.6	-1.2	0.6

Source: Jackson et al. (1997); Tables 3 and 4 above.

than Jackson et al. do. Expenditures on security, for example, to combat an increased fear of crime, count as adding to GDP, but serve only partly to cancel out the impact of crime on welfare. 50 per cent of both public and private spending on education and health is also excluded as being defensive. In the case of education this is because, it is argued, many qualifications are acquired merely to give a signal to potential employers (credentialisation) rather than to acquire genuine skills, and in the case of health it is because some spending is merely to counter the adverse effects of consumption elsewhere in the economy (such as smoking or pollution-related illnesses).

By far the most important parts of the adjustments are those to take account of resource depletion and environmental damage, which both exert a substantial downward pressure on the index. When all the adjustments are taken into account the ISEW is radically different from GDP. Table 5 compares the ISEW to GDP across the reference periods used earlier (except that the final period has had to be curtailed at 1996, which is the latest available data point for the index).

In stark contrast to GDP, which grew at an average annual rate of 2.5 per cent between 1953 and 1996, the ISEW increases only at a modest 0.9 per cent per annum. What is even more dramatic is the difference since 1977, where the ISEW has actually fallen in absolute terms to stand at a level in 1996 that is only 80 per cent of its 1977 value. Comparable estimates for other countries also show either a sharp levelling off or an absolute decline from the late 1970s onwards.

The idea that we should make adjustments to GDP to produce a broader estimate of economic welfare is reasonably uncontroversial. What is controversial is exactly how it is done. Several commentators have taken issue with the ISEW. Crafts in particular argues that the use of inequality as a component is inappropriate and that some value should be attached to the value of increased life expectancy, which he estimates was worth the equivalent of 1.3 per cent per annum GDP growth between 1950 and 1998.[22] With reference to income inequality, however, there is a simple statistical argument that GDP per head is a measure of mean income whereas what is a better measure of the increase in income of a typical person is the median. While we have no estimates of median GDP, it is interesting to note that in 1985 the ratio of median to mean net disposable income in the Family Expenditure Survey was 0.874; by 1998/9 it had fallen to 0.776. Adjusting for a change of this magnitude would knock 0.9 per cent per annum off GDP growth, which is actually rather more than the inequality adjustment made in the ISEW.

There are also many arguments about how things should be measured and what weight should be attached to them.[23] Taken as a whole, it does look as though the current ISEW has something of a downward bias, but it is a step towards answering the common question: 'How is it we are all wealthier, but do not feel any better off?' Just as important, it is also a useful attempt to make governments and the general population focus on broader issues rather than simply on GDP, which is a rather narrow measure of economic well-being.

The next 50 years

Economic forecasting is an imprecise art (even more imprecise than the exercise in historical economic accounting contained in the previous three sections of this chapter!) and any attempt to forecast what will happen over a 50-year period borders on the reckless. Nevertheless, using the framework in Table 1 we can begin to think about exactly how big the economy might be in 50 years' time.

The basic idea of Table 1 is that if we add together the growth rate of the population of working age, the effects of changes in labour markets, an allowance for the changing mix of full-time and part-time working, and productivity, we will get GDP growth. Of all these, the one area where we can establish a relatively firm view is demographics. Having said that, demographic projections are just that – projections. They are as subject to error as any other projections, particularly with respect to future birth rates and migration. Nevertheless, we tend to be happier using long-term projections of population change than we are using other long-term projections. The first two rows of Table 6 show the projected annual average changes in the population of working age[24] and the total population over the next 50 years.

To turn these into estimates of economic growth, following the methodology used in Table 1, we need to have a view of how the demographics relate to labour supply, of other labour market changes and future productivity growth. The trend in recent years has been for participation rates to fall, because of both an increase in higher education participation and an increase in early retirement. Neither of these trends is likely to continue indefinitely. With respect to early retirement, we are likely to see two conflicting phenomena. On the one hand, early retirement can be seen as income elastic. Consequently, as some people become better off, they are more likely to want to retire early. On the other hand, it is quite possible that, if pension provision fails to live up to expectations, the average age of retirement will increase. On the whole we are probably safe in making the 'neutral' assumption here that labour supply goes up in line with the population of working age.

The next step is to consider the potential for improving the efficiency of the labour market – in other words, the possibility of the NAIRU falling farther. Unemployment rates in the UK are still above their 1960s low, and conversely the ratio of employment to population adjusted for age-specific secular trends in participation is still well below its peak. This means that there is still some room for a contribution from the labour market. Even if employment rates were to return to the levels seen in the 1960s, however, this would only add 0.1 per cent per annum to employment and GDP growth over a 50-year period. The scope for generating growth through improved labour market efficiency is probably greater for the other large European economies, where employment rates are currently much lower than in the UK, but it will still be limited over such a long period.

This just leaves productivity growth, which is the most unpredictable and important of all the variables; relatively small increases in productivity can actually cancel out the adverse effects of ageing on GDP.[25] We have seen in Table 1, however, just how hard it is for UK productivity change to improve substantially. In the case of the USA the onset of the ICT revolution and a change in national accounting practice[26] had led many commentators to think that the economy had entered a 'new paradigm' of high productivity growth. The 'dot.com' crash, accounting scandals and data revisions have, however, exploded much of the US productivity miracle, and we should be cautious in making assumptions about future trends.

There may be some room for optimism in the UK. If we accept the 'batting average' argument as to why productivity growth has been disappointing over the last fifteen years, it is reasonable to assume that it will improve in the future as employment growth slows. A greater policy commitment to improving educational standards should also help. The other big European countries, on the other hand, may actually see some reduction in productivity growth if employment rates are improved, although Germany may do better as eastern Germany catches up over the period.

Putting all this together and making the modest assumptions that labour market changes contribute 0.1 per cent per annum to

Table 6 **Economic growth: the next 50 years?**
         (per cent per annum)

	UK	USA	Germany	France	Italy	Japan
Population	0.2	0.7	-0.3	0.1	-0.6	-0.3
Changing dependency rate	-0.2	-0.3	-0.4	-0.4	-0.6	-0.6
Population of working age	0.0	0.4	-0.7	-0.3	-1.2	-0.9
Labour market changes	0.1	0.0	0.2	0.2	0.2	0.0
Productivity	2.25	2.25	2.25	2.1	2.1	2.1
GDP	2.3	2.7	1.7	2.0	1.1	1.2
GDP/head	2.2	2.0	2.0	2.0	1.7	1.5
GDP, UK = 100	100	788	102	83	52	125
GDP/head, UK = 100	100	133	94	88	79	75

Source: Demographic data from the UN Medium Variant & National Statistics 2000-based population projections; other figures are illustrative assumptions.

growth in the UK over the next 50 years and 0.2 per cent to Germany, France and Italy, that labour productivity grows by 2.25 per cent per annum in the UK, USA and Germany and by 2.1 per cent elsewhere, we can sketch out a rough view of the relative size of the different economies in 50 years' time. The results, shown in Table 6, are of course driven largely by demographic considerations. Nevertheless, they are interesting. Under the assumptions outlined above, the UK is set to be the second fastest-growing economy of the six considered and the most rapid in terms of GDP per person.[27] Were this actually to happen, the USA would increase its size advantage over the other five but the UK would be neck and neck with the German economy in size and by 2051 would reach 80 per cent of the size of the Japanese economy. In terms of GDP per person, the UK would have clawed back some of the gap with the USA and would have a clear lead over the other five countries.

As well as being a speculative analysis, this is also very limited. By focusing on the large Western economies, we ignore the fact that smaller countries already top the GDP per person league table in Europe and the potential of newly industrialised countries, especially China. It is not, however, intended to be a comprehensive exercise, but rather one that can put into sharp focus the implications of current demographic projections for the economic position of the UK relative to that of major competitors over the next 50 years.

Nor does the methodology used in Table 6 take account of the arguments about sustainability and welfare outlined in the third section. Environmental policies are already high on many policy agendas and could adversely affect the rate of productivity growth (thought not the ISEW, hence the arguments for an alternative measure). The issue of income inequality could also be important. Increasing income inequality has gone hand in hand with improved output and employment growth since the mid-1980s. Policies aimed at reducing inequality could slow growth and, hence, there is an issue of the appropriate welfare trade-off between higher incomes and lower inequality.

Conclusions

This chapter has sketched out what has happened to economic growth over the past 50 years. In a limited space, there has been an inevitable skimping on detail, but the idea has been to show that things can and do change. The UK's seemingly inexorable relative economic decline appears to have been reversed and, going on the demographic projections at least, it may even leave some of its traditional competitors behind in the future. There again, the future can hold many surprises, and even the demographic projections are far from certain.

As they stand, our estimates show a near-threefold increase in GDP per head since 1951, followed by a similar increase over the next 50 years. The achievement of the past 50 years is no mean feat and, if repeated, would be an equally impressive illustration of what can be generated by market efficiency and technological change. Nevertheless, we can also question the relevance of GDP growth to well-being. The attraction of GDP is that it is relatively easy to measure. Concepts such as Sustainable Economic Welfare are currently crude and their composition debatable, but they do serve to widen the policy debate.

Notes

1   Research Director of Experian Business Strategies.
2   Organisation of Oil Exporting Countries, representing oil producers, mainly in the Middle East but also countries like Venezuela and Nigeria, most of whose production was exported; it does not include large producers such as the USA or former Soviet Union, most of whose production was consumed domestically – *Ed.*
3   In the 1980s the emphasis of macroeconomic policy in the UK, reflecting changes in economic ideas, shifted from managing demand, primarily by changes in tax and government spending, to focus instead on the control of inflation and greater reliance on monetary targeting. (See Chapters 3, 6 and 7 below – *Ed.*)
4   This was achieved by fitting a segmented time trend to the natural log of GDP and identifying a number of roughly equally spaced years that were close to the fitted trend. Both 1950 and 1951 were well above trend, while 1952 was well below it, so we have taken 1953 as the first benchmark; 2001 was actually marginally below trend (as defined here) but has still been used as a benchmark because of the convenience of having a final benchmark year that is as close to the present as possible.
5   The discouraged-worker effect is where individuals do not declare themselves as unemployed (and hence part of the labour force) because they do not think there is any chance of getting a job and/or they do not qualify for unemployment-related benefits.

6   N. F. R. Crafts, *Britain's Relative Economic Decline*, Institute of Economic Affairs, 2002.

7   Notwithstanding the impact of the late 1980s boom and early 1990s recession on macroeconomic stability, inflation has been lower and less variable than in the two preceding periods and there has been an absence of major international shocks on the scale of the oil-price shocks of 1973 and 1979.

8   Such as privatisation, enhanced competition policy, anti-union legislation, financial liberalisation and a run-down of interventionist industrial policies.

9   This is not so obvious in government-sponsored estimates based on extrapolating census data but is clear from a detailed analysis of the Labour Force Survey (Business Strategies Ltd, *Occupations in the Future*, London, 2001).

10 Interestingly growth in GDP per head between 1985 and 2001 was almost as high as in the Golden Age between 1953 and 1967. This is entirely due to the impact of the baby boom on the dependency rate in the earlier period. Since 1985 the fall in the share of the population below working age has actually slightly exceeded the impact of the growing numbers of retirement age to produce a small improvement (fall) in the dependency ratio.

11 Crafts, op. cit.

12 Tables 2–4 are based on GDP and population data from the IMF's International Financial Statistics data bank extended backwards where necessary by using data from A. Maddison, *The World Economy: A Millennial Perspective 1820–1992*, OECD, Paris, 2001, and updated using more recent national sources where available. The GDP data were converted to 2000 purchasing power standards (PPS) by multiplying through by the ratio of estimates of GDP in PPSs in 2000 (derived from European Commission, *European Economy No. 73*, Brussels, 2001) to the equivalent figure in local currency.

13 Because the economic cycles of different economies are often not synchronous, international comparisons of this type can be affected by the choice of benchmark years. None of the

benchmark years chosen here causes particularly large distortions. If we were to choose 2000 as the final benchmark year and omit 2001, which was a slow year for growth in Germany, Japan and the USA, the growth rankings for the last period would not be affected.

14   Crafts, op. cit.

15   The System of National Accounts 1993 and the European System of Accounts 1995, also known as SNA(93) and ESA(95).

16   A. Bassanini and S. Scarpetta, *The Driving Forces of Economic Growth: Panel Data Evidence for the OECD Countries*, OECD Economic Studies No. 33, OECD, Paris, 2002.

17   GDP, like many economic statistics, is subject to a number of measurement and conceptual problems. Apart from difficulties in measurement when we are comparing estimates over time, we need to allow for changes in prices. This is problematic when the mix of goods being produced is very different at different points in time.

18   M. L. Weitzman, 'Pricing the Limits to Growth from Mineral Depletion', *Quarterly Journal of Economics*, May 1999.

19   H. Daly and J. Cobb, *For the Common Good – Redirecting the Economy towards Community, the Environment and Sustainable Economic Development*, Beacon Press, Boston, MA, 1989.

20   H. Diefenbacher , 'The Index of Sustainable Economic Welfare in Germany', in C. and J. Cobb (eds), *The Green National Product*, University Press of America, Lanham, MD, 1994. See also T. Jackson, J. Marks, J. Ralls and S. Stymne, *Sustainable Economic Welfare in the UK, 1950–1996*, Centre for Environmental Strategy, University of Surrey, Guildford, 1997.

21   Also known as the Genuine Progress Indicator (GPI) in some countries.

22   Crafts, op. cit. See also N. F. R. Crafts, 'The Human Development Index and Changes in the Standard of Living', *European Review of Economic History*, vol. 1, no. 3, 1997, pp. 300–22.

23   The Friends of the Earth website, www.foe.co.uk/campaigns/

sustainable_development/progress/, even lets you calculate your own ISEW by varying the weights used.

24   Working age is defined for the UK as 16–64 for men and 16–59 for women. No account has been taken of the scheduled increase in the state retirement age for women. For other countries, because of limited data availability, working age is defined as 15–59.

25   D. Cutler, J. Porterba, L. Sheiner and L. Summers, 'An Ageing Society: Opportunity or Challenge?', *Brookings Papers on Economic Activity*, 1990:1, pp. 1–75.

26   The introduction of chain linking to estimate constant-price GDP.

27   The forecast growth rate in GDP per head of 2.2 per cent in the UK is rather more than the 1.3 per cent projected in G. Young, 'Ageing and the UK Economy', *Bank of England Quarterly Bulletin*, vol. 42, no. 3, 2002. However, his projections assume quite a modest growth in the capital stock and in labour productivity. The projection here is for a 290 per cent increase in GDP per head over the 50-year period.

3

THE RISE AND FALL OF INFLATION

Roger Bootle[1]

Inflation is now low nearly everywhere, and the signs are that this is set to remain the norm for many years to come. Indeed, if this regime is to be challenged in the years ahead it is more likely, in my view, to be through the experience of deflation than the return to the high inflation of the 1970s. Yet most business economists practising their calling over the last 30 years have worked in a very different world, and until very recently to have suggested that an inflation rate of 2–3 per cent per annum should be assumed as a central case for business planning purposes would have risked confirming all the bosses' worst fears about economics and economists. Are we now to regard the great post-war inflation as simply the product of a unique period in history? Or will inflation come back and bite us some time soon?

Longer historical experience

Clearly post-war inflation did not emerge into a world previously inexperienced in this phenomenon. Throughout history there have been bouts of severe inflation which have played havoc with money's value, and indeed at times virtually destroyed it. For monetary systems using coins made of precious metal, such as gold, the main inflationary risk has always been a deliberate reduction in the precious metal content of the coins below their official value. There is evidence of such debasement as far back as classical Greece.

In the monetary system introduced throughout the Roman world by the Emperor Augustus, the face value of coins was at first closely related to the value of the metallic content. Subsequently, however, as public spending increased beyond the capacity of the tax system to finance it, the silver denarius was debased. Over the third century, money may have fallen to a fiftieth of its value at the beginning. Under the Emperor Diocletian there was even an attempt to impose a wage and price freeze throughout the empire.

The first country to use paper money seems to have been China – as noted by Marco Polo. Moreover, China had early experience of quite serious inflation. From 1190 to 1240, the price level rose by more than twenty times, or at an annual rate of more than 6 per cent.

Despite these episodes of inflation in the past, the historical record also shows some long periods of overall price stability. In Britain, the price level seems to have been more or less the same at the beginning of the sixteenth century as it was at the beginning of the fourteenth century. Moreover, after the long period of quite high inflation in the sixteenth century, there was a very long period of overall price stability which lasted to the very eve of our own era. Indeed, in 1932 prices in Britain were slightly *lower* than they had been in 1795.

The world's most spectacular experiences with inflation came in the twentieth century. Between 1919 and 1925, five European countries suffered hyperinflation – Austria, Hungary, Poland, Russia and Germany. The record for the highest rate, however, is held by the *second* Hungarian inflation, of 1945–6, when the rate was 19,800 per cent *per month*. The unifying theme running through all these inflationary episodes is the coincidence of weak governments and bad times, often as a result of war or its aftermath.

Inflation after 1945

The 1930s, of course, were years of depression and high unemployment, not inflation. Nevertheless, looking back, one can see the seeds of post-war inflation in the attenuated fall of money wages and prices in the face of weak demand. Whatever stopped prices and wages from falling when demand was weak could readily cause prices to rise when demand was only a little stronger. Moreover, in conditions where some parts of the economy were experiencing very strong demand and others weak demand, price rises in the first would not be offset by price falls in the second. This would cause the overall price level to edge up.

So it proved. After World War II, inflation became ingrained as the norm everywhere in the industrial world. During the Korean War there was a brief inflationary upsurge, which took inflation in the USA above 9 per cent in 1951. After this, however, the rate of inflation subsided. In the 1950s as a whole, inflation averaged 2 per cent in the USA, just over 1 per cent in Germany and just over 4 per cent in Britain. And it remained quite low until the late 1960s.

What makes the first 25 years after the war so remarkable from a current perspective is that low inflation was not bought at the expense of high unemployment or slow growth. Quite the opposite. Growth was rapid and sustained, and unemployment was maintained at unprecedentedly low levels. In the USA, it fell throughout the 1960s. In many ways, these years look like a golden age.

But by the late 1960s, the warning bells were already ringing for the regime of strong growth accompanied by steady, low inflation. In a number of European countries, there were severe civil disturbances and labour unrest in 1968. And in Italy there was unrest and wage militancy in the 'hot autumn of 1969'. In most of the industrial world, the trade-off between inflation and unemployment seemed to be deteriorating.

Then, in the early 1970s, three partly related shocks nearly brought the industrial world to its knees. The first was the collapse, in 1971, of the fixed exchange-rate system which had operated

since the end of the war.[2] The world staggered towards a new
system of floating exchange rates.

In many countries, the end of fixed exchange rates was thought
to remove an unnecessary shackle on domestic economic policy.
In 1972–3 there was an upsurge in commodity prices, which then
fed back into the inflationary process in the developed economies.
Measured by *The Economist* Commodity Price Index, in dollar
terms, non-oil commodity prices rose by nearly 30 per cent in
1972, by more than 60 per cent in 1973, and by more than 20 per
cent in 1974.

Yet for all the potential importance of the rise in commodity
prices in causing inflation in the early 1970s, it probably does not
constitute a wholly *independent* explanation for the inflationary
upsurge in the early 1970s. For although the commodity price
explosion was perceived in the West as a supply shock, and although it was partly associated with the effects on food production
of bad weather in the USA and elsewhere, it was also partly a result
of the rapid increase in world *demand* and industrial production.

The same cannot be said, however, of the much more important
shock which appeared in late 1973 – the dramatic hike in oil prices.
It is difficult to exaggerate the impact that this had on costs, prices,
expectations and economic management. For the industrial West,
it was comparable, in economic terms, to the outbreak of war. The
West had been used to remarkable stability in oil prices for a very
long time – until these prices went through the roof in 1973.

According to one viewpoint, the increase in oil prices was
simply another manifestation of the worldwide boom, and as such
is of no particular importance analytically. In practice, though, it
is difficult to sustain this view. For a start, the magnitude of the
rise in oil prices – sixfold from 1972 to 1974 – cannot plausibly be
pinned on an increase in demand for oil, not least given the history
of the oil price since the end of the war and the way in which the
price was increased, as a result of production cutbacks instituted
by the producer cartel, OPEC,[3] in the wake of the Arab–Israeli
conflict.

Nevertheless, there is still an important question to ask – why should the rise in oil prices (or indeed the earlier increase in non-oil commodity prices) have produced an upsurge in inflation rather than simply a shift in relative prices? After all, monetarist economists would argue that as long as the money supply was held constant, a rise in some prices would be offset by a fall in others. Their case is that it was a major increase in the money supply which caused the upsurge of inflation. (According to the monetarists, it always is.)

There are several reasons why a sharp rise in the price of oil could not simply cause a shift in relative prices. The importance of the commodity in question and the ubiquity of its use throughout the industrial world, combined with the sheer size of the price increase, meant that the rise in oil prices effected a substantial worsening in the terms of trade for industrial countries which was bound to imply a substantial fall in their real incomes, the brunt of which would have to fall on consumers. In the circumstances, the only way the overall price level could be held constant was for wages to fall in nominal terms. In practice, however, in most countries workers were unprepared to accept the falls in their real wages implied by higher oil prices, let alone falls in *nominal* wages.

Indeed, what workers would have had to accept in order to prevent inflation was more demanding than what was expected of them in the late 1920s and early 1930s. At that time prices were falling, with the result that real incomes were rising. Even then, as we saw above, workers were extremely resistant to pay cuts. After 1973, far from accepting cuts in nominal incomes, workers pushed pay up. A struggle over relative real incomes occurred as governments, companies and groups of workers fought to preserve their share of a diminished cake.

Moreover, the very visibility and ubiquity of the price rises caused by the oil-price hike led people to increase their inflationary expectations, thereby exacerbating the inflation itself. It cannot be emphasised enough how shocking the upsurge of inflation was at the time. The US Consumer Price Index, which had risen by only 3.4 per cent in 1972, rose by 8.8 per cent in 1973 and 12.2 per cent in 1974.

The swing to disinflation

The oil shock presented policy-makers with an acute policy dilemma. For it was a double-edged blow. To the oil-consuming countries (which meant most of the industrial West) the rise in the oil price was both *inflationary* of prices and *deflationary* of real demand. The higher prices paid for oil reduced real incomes and therefore tended to reduce consumption. Yet the oil producers were unlikely to spend their new-found riches. Accordingly, there would be a slump in demand which would cause higher unemployment. Should the world's monetary authorities respond to the higher inflation and tighten policy, thereby worsening the upward pressure on unemployment? Or should they respond to the upward pressure on unemployment by easing policy, hence risking higher inflation?

Under the weight of the prevailing, Keynesian,[4] orthodoxy of the time, which emphasised the overriding importance of combating unemployment and downplayed the significance of inflation, most governments chose the latter course. Even so, they soon discovered that they still had to endure a large rise in unemployment, alongside very high inflation.

The scene was set for a sharp change in the policy regime. The roots of this change lay in the same phenomenon which had caused the sharp change of policy regime before World War II. Under the gold standard, economic policy was dominated by the need to maintain a certain fixed link to gold; during the first 35 years after the war it was dominated by the need to maintain unemployment at a low level. This is what Sir John Hicks called the labour standard. What had destroyed the gold standard was the unacceptably high unemployment costs of deflation in conditions where pay and prices had become institutionalised and subject to producer power. But in the crises of the 1970s these self-same conditions then destroyed the labour standard, by producing unacceptably high rates of inflation.

When a second oil-price shock in 1979 threatened to produce similar results to the 1973–4 experience, the prevailing reaction of governments and central banks throughout the Western world was now very different. In view of the experience of the rapid inflation of the mid-1970s, this time round the response more or less everywhere was to try to resist the inflationary upsurge by the use of high real short-term interest rates.

With inflation initially very high, this meant very high nominal short rates. In the USA, the Federal Reserve under Paul Volcker at times drove interest rates up to 17 per cent during 1980, and even to 19 per cent in 1981. Furthermore, *long* interest rates (yields) rose sharply as well since investors were reluctant to buy bonds. It is as though, having been caught by the high inflation of the 1970s for which they were unprepared, and having thereby been rewarded with negligible or even negative real returns, bond investors now set out to make up for lost time.

This change of policy compared to the first oil-price shock, and the preparedness to accept serious recession and unemployment as its consequence, marked a turning point in the history of inflation in the post-war period. It reflected a profound change in the intellectual climate, as well as a marked change in society's attitude towards inflation and unemployment.

Among the public at large, there was a corresponding change. Without knowing anything of inflation/unemployment trade-offs, many people experienced alarm at the high inflation and instability of the 1970s. This was reflected electorally in a marked shift to the right which brought in conservative administrations in the USA, Britain and elsewhere. When, despite the serious recession and unemployment produced by anti-inflationary policy, these conservative administrations were subsequently re-elected, the change of voter preferences was apparently confirmed.

The policy revolution spread farther. In the early 1980s, under President Mitterrand, France tried to resist the tide and carried on with a policy directed towards maintaining high employment. But eventually it buckled in the face of the strain. Indeed, its volte-face was nothing less than extraordinary, for having tried to go it alone in pursuit of the old orthodoxy, it later decided, in the shape of the *franc fort* policy, to try to be more German than the Germans in pursuit of the new orthodoxy. The result was inflation in France running below that in Germany, but also unemployment stuck at very high levels.

Another boom at the end of the 1980s saw a short-term upswing in inflation, again resisted by high interest rates. For those countries that were members of the European Exchange Rate Mechanism (ERM), real interest rates were kept up by the peg to German nominal interest rates, which themselves were kept high in order to bear down on the high rates of inflation that followed the boom of the late 1980s and the excesses of German re-unification. France was the most extreme case, with real interest rates at one point approaching 10 per cent.

By contrast, the 1990s was a decade of low inflation almost everywhere. Within Europe, for many countries the efforts to adopt the euro, and the subsequent handing over of monetary policy to an independent central bank in Frankfurt, have transformed a historical record of high inflation into a current reality of very low inflation.

In much, though not all, of Europe this continues to be accompanied by weak growth and high unemployment. But elsewhere, the signs of a real transformation have emerged as low inflation is combined with low unemployment. This is the story in the USA and the UK. Given significant reform of the labour market, it may well be the story in the eurozone as well.

The lessons of history

So what can we learn from the historical record on inflation? Inflation is caused by the struggle between different groups within society over their share of national income. In a sense, therefore, it results from a malfunctioning of the political system.

Classic monetary inflation fits nicely into this framework. Governments cause inflation when they try, by manipulating the currency, to secure more of the national income than they are willing or able to finance openly through taxation.

Once a metallic standard is replaced by paper money, then the power of governments to create inflation is increased enormously. But simultaneously, without the anchor provided by a metallic standard, the power of the private banking system to increase the money supply is also unleashed. The possibility of a credit inflation opens up, where it is not competition for resources between the public and private sectors which causes the inflation, but rather competition between different parts of the private sector. Central banks have still been able to control this inflation through interest rate policy, and sometimes through restrictions on bank lending. But this has been control at arm's length.

The sort of inflation we have experienced in the post-war period reflects a further stage in historical development – the upsurge of producer power, which led to battles between producer groups for shares of the cake, battles in which the role of monetary factors, although supportive, was secondary.

The increases in oil prices in 1973 and 1979 can also be seen within this framework. They represented the exercise of producer power on an international scale. They imposed a substantial real income loss (corresponding to OPEC's gain) on all the industrial countries that were not self-sufficient in energy. This unleashed a struggle within society over who should bear the loss.

Future prospects

Business economists are often required to foretell the future, yet they know only too well the limitations of their tools. These are evident enough with regard to short-term forecasting, so presumably the difficulties should be greater for periods of a decade or more over which a business might reasonably consider planning its future. There is a powerful temptation to recoil and take refuge in the defence that there is nothing that economists can say. But again that is something which our employers are liable to find unimpressive.

What reasons are there for believing that inflation will stay low in the future? The period when producer power (including the power of organised labour) was a major inflationary source can be regarded as a phase in economic development. But this phase is now ending. The world is becoming super-competitive, thanks to technical change and globalisation. This is creating a series of favourable price shocks and inhibiting producer groups from trying to seize increased shares of the cake.

Second, at just the time that, because of this, the environment has become disinflationary, central banks and governments have acquired a dedication to low inflation. This is a deadly combination – deadly for inflation, that is.

Nevertheless, the cynics say that this is just a temporary phenomenon. Upsurges of excessive demand prompted by lax policy are to be expected as a matter of course, because democratic governments will regularly succumb to the temptation to gain popularity. Bursts of inflation are simply the inevitable outcome of the interaction between democratic politics and paper money.

In my opinion, this view does not do justice to the workings of democratic politics in advanced societies – and also does a fair bit of violence to the facts. For the countries of the industrial West, at least, the macroeconomic temptations facing politicians can easily be exaggerated. After the experience of the 1970s, inflation is not popular with the voters. So it is by no means obvious that politicians win elections by distributing fiscal largesse or opening the monetary floodgates. And just for the record, in the post-war period the countries with the highest inflation are *not* the industrial democracies but rather developing countries with only limited democracy, military dictatorships or totalitarian regimes.

The recent change of attitude by democratic governments and central banks towards inflation is usually regarded as completely separate from the intensification of competition through globalisation which is such a dominant influence on business. But it can be viewed usefully as the product of the same forces. Because of the information and communication revolution, as well as the effects of deregulation, governments (and central banks) can control much less than they used to be able to. Meanwhile, their financial and economic stewardship, particularly with regard to debt and currency values, is closely scrutinised by well-informed, sophisticated, global financial markets, which are able to give an adverse verdict at the drop of a hat.

As a result, however immune they may be to competition within their own countries, governments and central banks are now seen by the markets to be in competition with each other. The result is that they can get away with very little. The costs of an inflationary strategy are quickly apparent and, for any rational, responsible government, this serves to deter the attempt.

Thus, not only the powerful corporations and labour unions, but even the ultimate repository of producer power – the state provider of money itself and of economic management – is now being tamed by globalisation.

Another act?

When the economist is forced to forecast the unforecastable it is customary to rely on a simple but robust assumption. With regard to inflation the temptation is to assume that the current regime will continue. So it is perfectly respectable simply to suggest inflation carrying on at the current targeted rate, namely 2.5 per cent per annum.

Yet reasonable and understandable though this is, it is far from satisfactory, bearing in mind the tortuous route by which we arrived at this point, and the peculiar arbitrariness of the 2.5 per cent figure. I suspect that the play has another act to come. If so, a major player in it is going to be the re-emergence of deflation.

A few years ago, if you espoused this view you were widely believed to be mad. (Believe me, I know.) After the experience of continued deflation in Japan and the stock market collapse of the last three years, however, it is no longer regarded as absurd to take deflation seriously. Nevertheless, most people who have ever considered it, including most economists, still find it incredible. Typically they have a knee-jerk response – the policy-makers will stop it.

I find this idea unsatisfactory and unconvincing. It derives from the textbook lesson that a government acting in cahoots with its central bank has no limits on the quantity of its own money it can create, and it can therefore always escape from deflation by turning the printing presses.

But we do not live in a textbook world – even though many academic economists give the impression that they have never stepped outside one. For a start, there is the problem of correctly spotting the deflationary forces sufficiently far in advance to take action, and then taking sufficient action to head them off. With the world's central bankers still worried about inflation (even in Japan) and still apparently of the view that interest rates are highly effective tools (except in Japan), they are liable to do too little, too late.

Once deflation is established in the mind then, like inflation, it can be devilishly difficult to dislodge. Yes, of course, given an infinite amount of monetary stimulus, deflation can be stopped. But governments do not dispose of infinite amounts of anything. They have to decide how much and in what form. In practice, they are likely to want to get away with not very much because a policy of extreme monetary stimulus would have costs and side effects, not least the danger that it would ultimately go too far and cause rampant inflation. Moreover, it would potentially cause instability in exchange rates which could threaten international relations. (This has been a key concern for the Japanese authorities. They have been particularly worried about the effects of a weak yen on relations with China and the United States.)

So my suspicion is that given sufficient weakness of aggregate demand, emanating perhaps from the recent collapse of asset values, the countries of the industrial West could easily slip into mild deflation and initially the monetary authorities would be unable to stop it. Germany may be the country most at risk since it has no independent monetary policy of its own.

They may even end up having to be tolerant of it. One of the most worrying aspects of the approach to setting interest rates driven by consumer price inflation, which has been pursued over recent years, is that it assists the inflation of asset-price bubbles. Once it becomes clear how serious the effects of the recent bubble were, then on both sides of the Atlantic we may move towards a policy framework designed to prevent this happening again.

Now if you support the raising of interest rates to prick a financial bubble even though inflation remains very low, then you must accept the risk of sending the inflation rate negative in order to achieve your aim. The objective would presumably be broad stability, including consumer price stability, over the medium term. But this would necessarily entail some *in*stability for the price level, both up and down, in the short term.

I know that we are not there yet and the policy-makers are full of reasons why they should not pursue such a policy. But I am trying to look ahead. If something like this were to happen then it would represent the final demise of post-war inflation, and a return to something like the regime of fluctuating prices which existed before the war.

Whether that would be a good thing or a bad thing is another question.

Notes

1   Managing Director, Capital Economics; Fellow of the Society of Business Economists.

2   The Bretton Woods arrangements. See Note 5, Chapter 1 – *Ed.*

3   See Note 2, Chapter 2 – *Ed.*

4   See Note 6, Chapter 1, and Chapter 7 – *Ed.*

4

ENVIRONMENT AND BUSINESS: SOCIALLY RESPONSIBLE BUT PRIVATELY PROFITABLE?

David Pearce[1]

Models of the firm

Economics, as it is practised in schools and universities, still teaches that corporations exist to make as much profit as possible. It is easy to see why this would be the case if the owners and managers of the corporation were one and the same. Managers would be in business to generate profits that accrued to themselves as the shareholders. Once management becomes divorced from ownership – the advent of 'managerial capitalism' – the coincidence of ownership and management goals no longer holds. Managers may pursue any number of objectives, but the extent to which they are allowed to deviate from maximising profits will be constrained by shareholder pressure. All kinds of incentive mechanisms exist to get the managers (the 'agents') to act in the interests of the shareholders (the 'principals') – such as profit-related bonuses and management shareholdings. The extent to which these principal-agent mechanisms are successful determines the degree of flexibility that managers have to pursue non-profit goals. These goals might include social or political recognition, 'empire-building' (focusing on turnover rather than profits), and the achievement of personal ethical concerns such as protecting the environment and benefiting the local community. These non-profit goals are sometimes summarised as 'managerial utility' – some measure of managerial well-being that is not wholly linked to making profits.

Some commentators have taken the view that *public* corporations always were socially accountable because their charters were originally subject to the interests of the Crown. Hence, as Will Hutton says, their 'licence to trade comes with the reciprocal public responsibilities to the communities within which they do business'.[2] But whatever the historical intent, the fact is that corporations lost this 'public good' characteristic some considerable time ago, as Hutton acknowledges.

In recent years, a substantial effort has been made by social and environmental pressure groups to encourage, cajole and even legally oblige corporations to become more socially responsible, to act more in the interests of the natural environment and the relatively deprived in society. But corporate social responsibility (CSR) has become more than a slogan of persuasion. Governments have sought to capitalise on CSR as a means of 'soft' regulation – regulation that gets corporations to self-regulate rather than having heavy-handed legislation imposed on them. So, a few years into the 21st century we have a somewhat odd mixture of pressures determining corporate goals: the traditional, and unquestionably still very powerful, goal of making profits; non-profit managerial goals that have simply grown with the divorce of principals and agents; demands by non-governmental organisations (NGOs), and some 'ethical' fund-holders, that corporations be more like social institutions than profit-maximisers; and governmental exploitation of the corporate social responsibility movement. The question is: which goal is best going to describe future corporations? Are we witnessing the transition to corporations as social enterprises, or is corporate social responsibility a passing fashion?

Certainly, corporations have become more environmentally and socially sensitive over the past 50 years or so. As this chapter shows, the explanations for this change are disputed, ranging from the view that corporations are now managed by managers who genuinely have environmental goals as part of their management strategy, to views that suggest environmental responsibility is a low-cost means of accommodating increasing external pressures. Either way, the list of initiatives in this field is impressive. Many companies now produce environmental reports or environmental statements, and some produce social reports as well, each describing the corporation's impacts on the local and national environment and on communities, the goals they seek to achieve, and progress in achieving these goals. 'Sustainability reporting' has naturally followed, but it seems fair to say that most of these reports suffer a lack of clear definition of the meaning of sustainability. Efforts to standardise sustainability reports – such as the Global Reporting Initiative (GRI)[3] – focus on selected indicators, but similarly lack a rigorous grounding in a model of sustainable development. Most of this reporting is voluntary but has been aided by the development of environmental management systems under an EU regulation made in 1993. This regulation established, and has subsequently revised, the eco-management and audit scheme (EMAS).[4] Leading companies also seek to achieve the ISO14001 international environmental standard for reporting as the dominant form of an EMAS. These systems imply continual improvement in environmental standards.

The development of external pressures on corporations to behave in a more socially responsible manner has also been rapid. It is clear that some governments have viewed social responsibility as a means of offloading the regulatory task to corporations. Some of this pressure has taken the form of exhortatory measures – the European Union's Green Paper on CSR,[5] for example – but some has mandated regulators to insist on social responsibility as part of corporations' required behaviour (the position taken in the UK Utilities Act, for example). To a considerable extent, governments have ridden on the backs of pressures from other sources, notably ethical investment funds, and especially those managed by pension schemes. Inevitably, a whole host of indicators and league tables have followed, such as the FTSE4Good Index. Even the laws governing corporate behaviour have raised the profile of environmental and social performance. The review of company law in the UK has suggested that companies consider such perfor-mance within the normal remit of financial and operational review. The 1995 Pensions Act requires that trustees make a dec-laration about social, environmental and ethical considerations in their Statement of Investment Principles. The number of initia-tives both within and outside the corporate sector is almost endless. But while the picture is a confusing one, the sheer existence of so many activities dedicated to reforming the profit-maximising model of the corporation must be seen as evidence of change away from 'profits only' to the corporation as social enter-prise. The questions remain: why has this all happened, and does it really constitute a departure from the traditional model of the firm as profit-maximiser?

Social enterprise as natural evolution

One response to this question is 'does it matter?' First, if the socially responsible firm is part of a natural evolution of business, it is unclear why anyone should want to change it. Put another way, if all the players – shareholders, managers, NGOs and government – are happy to see things change towards social enterprise, why is there a problem? From a social standpoint, all that is happening is that corporations are swapping one form of benefit – shareholder profits – for, say, environmental improvement. So long as no one is being coerced, society as a whole is better off. Some would go even further and say that social responsibility actually *comple-ments* profit-making. The greater the corporate effort towards social goals, the higher the market rewards that corporation secures. This 'win-win' outcome comes about either through very simple complementarities – saving energy benefits the environ-ment and saves costs too – or through somewhat more complex interactions. An example of the latter might be the fact that, where before firms with large environmental liabilities – potential de-commissioning or clean-up costs, for example – might have got away with ignoring them, or playing them down, today they have to treat them as real costs because of the threat of litigation or plain bad publicity.

Much of the CSR literature pursues this 'win-win' argument. If 'win-win' were true, then the question raised about the future social profile of the corporation would remain interesting, but politically redundant. Firms will pursue social responsibility and in doing so will make higher long-term profits than they would have done otherwise. Perhaps they will secure some market share from 'green consumers' – the success of organic produce might be cited in support of this view. Perhaps employees, as well as consumers, have socially responsible preferences, so that retaining a trained labour force requires behaving as employees would expect.

But 'win-win' relies on there being substantial and pervasive cost inefficiencies in the corporate sector. The picture is of an entire managerial class unaware that it is losing money by not taking the environment or social concerns seriously. No doubt there are many inefficiencies of this kind. We know that lines of information within corporations are often such that directors may be unaware of the firm's energy bill, or its environmental liabili-ties. But to suggest that these inefficiencies are widespread and significant in profit terms is not credible, despite the ever-expand-ing list of books claiming otherwise. It is far more likely that the inefficiencies are being spotted and corrected and that there is a rising cost curve involved in further improving energy and environmental efficiency. The argument is not that these ineffi-ciencies do not exist, but that their removal is not as costless an ex-ercise as the 'win-win' advocates would have us believe.

Social responsibility may improve profitability in ways other than through cost reductions. Prima facie, the surest way to test the proposition that CSR is good for profit is to see whether cor-porations meeting some CSR standard outperform those corpora-tions that do not. Unfortunately, many commentators appear to have been seduced into thinking that this correlation is *all* that is needed to establish that CSR is 'good for profits'. For the 'CSR equals more profits' view to be correct it must be the case, first, that corporations with good social performance also have good profit performance, and, second, that their good performance is *due to* being socially responsible. Much of the evidence adduced for the view that CSR *causes* higher profitability comes from stock exchange performance indicators. There are many examples. Thus the Dow Jones Sustainability Group Index out-performed the Global Index between 1995 and 2000. The Domini 400 Social Index has outperformed the Dow and Standard and Poors indices since it was launched in 1990. But the presumption behind these statements is that outperformance is *due to* being socially responsible. The presumption seems reasonable since factors other than social responsibility should be common to the market's valuation of all corporations. But correlation is not causality. In the absence of stronger statistical tests that relate per-formance to all the factors that are likely to determine it, it is wise to be cautious before jumping to the conclusion that statistical cor-relation implies causal connection.

Hence the evidence that the market capitalises social responsi-bility into profits or share prices is not very persuasive. Some studies find in favour, some do not. But even if the balance of empirical evidence were in favour, it is far more likely that what is being seen is first-mover advantage. Some corporations have been adept at promoting an environmental or social image, often for very modest efforts. They may have gained market share, social goodwill and even higher share prices as a result. But would that trend prevail if all corporations followed suit? There also has to be a deep suspicion that empirical findings of the coincidence of high profits and social responsibility reflect not the influence of CSR on profits but the influence of good management. Put another way, what high profit and socially responsible firms have in common is a particular form of management. CSR alone will not generate profits.

The meaning and genesis of corporate social responsibility

What is it that corporations are supposed to be signing up to by becoming 'socially responsible'? The World Business Council for Sustainable Development declares corporate social responsibility to be: 'The commitment of business to contribute to sustainable economic development, working with employees, their families, the local community and society at large to improve their quality of life.'

This is sufficiently vague to be consistent with most corporate activity. More demanding have been the agencies providing more precise lists of do's and don'ts. One industry that has grown up is the 'accreditation' industry, akin to that which accompanied environmental impact statements, and environmental and social reporting. Since corporations' own claims to be socially responsible cannot be taken at face value, such claims have to be accredited by independent agencies. These may be environmental or business consultants or, increasingly, the accreditation can be bought by appointing representatives of NGOs to advisory committees or even board membership. The commitment is then to whatever these individuals and bodies regard as social responsibility. The more powerful accreditors, however, have emerged as organisations that can give a market rating for corporations. Simply to get on to the relevant list is then an achievement, while rising up the ranking is a subsequent goal. The interesting feature of these developments is the extent to which they are self-fulfilling. Once a list exists, there is no point in arguing that the list measures the wrong things. What matters is getting on the list. CSR is whatever the accreditors say it is. There are no signs that such lists have evolved from a careful comparison of the costs and benefits of meeting the list's criteria. Curiously, too, the criteria are invariably non-quantitative – a successful corporation has to do something but it is far from clear how much of it they have to do.

What accounts for the rise of CSR doctrine? One suggestion is that CSR reflects a wider challenge to traditional materialist values. Various social surveys have found that income and happiness may be correlated only up to a point because income is seen as a means of securing a job, healthcare (in nations without social health services), a home and old-age security. Beyond this, income growth does not produce any more happiness. Perhaps what is happening is that people recognise that increases in consumption are at the cost of reductions in 'social capital' (sense of community, trust, social bonds), reductions in environmental quality, and even reduced choices between work and leisure. A common feature of the 'richer is not happier' surveys is the relative deprivation concept. Happiness, it is suggested, derives from being better off relative to some reference group in society. But if incomes rise generally, then while we are all better off in absolute terms, nothing has happened to the relativities, and hence none of us is any happier despite the growth in income.

One suggestion is that the 'social corporation' is simply a manifestation of the change in social preferences away from material things towards communal and social goods. There is some evidence that there have been 'value shifts' towards more 'post-materialist' views of the world. This might suggest that future prospects for sustainable development are brighter because the value changes favour more social and environmental trends and less emphasis on material consumption. This should be true if social and political institutions are sensitive to such changes. There would then be only a limited case for engineering social change to bring environmental policies about – they will occur naturally as post-material values grow to dominate material values. CSR would be a manifestation of this change. A second view observes that the changes in values have not been accompanied by changes in the ways economies are organised, so that what does make people happy is what gets increasingly supplied. If post-materialism is a strong force, and CSR is one outcome of it, one would expect dramatically more evidence that CSR is emerging as a strong corporate response. Yet the evidence is that only a tiny fraction of corporations report the environmental and social impacts of their activities. This suggests that post-materialists have experienced difficulties in getting their views across, or that they simply lack the political power to influence social change. Certainly, some commentators believe that post-materialists lack power because there are vested interests in securing more economic growth, interests that have been enhanced by globalisation of the world economy. On this analysis, then, there is a constant struggle between those with goals of happiness and those with goals of increased consumption.

Taking the evidence on social value change and happiness trends at their face values, there remains a mystery. If social value change is occurring, it appears to result in only very modest institutional change. Hence, either those adopting the value changes are not powerful, or something else is happening. The something else could be the relative income argument whereby people are caught up in an endless spiral of increasing material desires even though they appear to know it will not make them happier. Either way – limited power or uncontrollable spiral – on this analysis the future for CSR would not appear to be a strong one.

Social enterprise as a trade-off against profits

The evidence is not easy to evaluate, but what there is suggests not the 'win-win' model of social responsibility, but a trade-off model in which, at least beyond a point, serving the goals of social responsibility sacrifices shareholder returns. Again, if this is the result of evolutionary forces occurring within the corporate governance process, so be it. Society may be as well off with this trend as without it. But a number of economic commentators suspect that social responsibility is being forced on corporations against their better judgement, and this process of coercion has a cost in terms of profits. In turn, lost profits mean lost jobs and lost output. Again, the degree of social coercion may be 'optimal': if corporations refuse to undertake the 'right' amount of environmental protection and to produce the 'right' level of care for the community, then coercion is justified. This would be the traditional argument for regulation, namely that profit-maximisers will not voluntarily internalise the external costs their activities impose on society. Hence they must be made to do it. The reason that some people doubt whether the observed level of coercion is indeed optimal is because it appears not to be the outcome of any rational balancing of costs and benefits. Rather it is imposed by implicit threat. An environmental movement may threaten to boycott a corporation that does not do its will, or to provide other adverse publicity. Examples abound of such conduct. Moreover, these demands for social responsibility all occur on top of the prevailing raft of legislation designed to get corporations to internalise externalities, from energy taxes to direct regulations.

If trade-offs exist, why have corporations acceded to many of the demands for CSR? Various suggestions can be made.

First, if first-movers genuinely gain from adopting CSR, they will willingly adopt these goals. What may be happening is that we are observing the first tranche of socially responsible actions, with later tranches being less likely to come about as the trade-offs become more severe.

Second, acceding to CSR demands may be good business if the alternative is a world in which pressure groups harass non-complying corporations. Few corporations now actively challenge environmentalist demands, for example, and some that have have lived to rue the day. A 'quiet life' is better than a confrontational one. Both may be at the expense of profits. A variation on this explanation is that corporations are accepting self-regulation in the expectation that it will preclude future direct governmental regulation which they (and, for that matter, government) regard as being more costly. For this to be a good explanation there must be some implicit 'contract' between government and business, something that is hard to prove but to which the rise of voluntary agreements lends some support.

Third, as argued by David Henderson,[6] so long as a few key corporations take on the CSR mantle and incur costs in doing so, they then have a direct interest in ensuring that all their competitors face the same cost increases by also becoming socially responsible. This does not explain why the initial few acceded to CSR demands, but it is probable that the 'quiet life' argument has a lot to do with it. Certainly, Henderson's arguments offer some explanation for the emergence of business organisations that themselves advocate and disseminate CSR.

Fourth, and less widely countenanced, CSR advocates may be being hoodwinked by the business sector. Corporations can be masters of making small gestures appear like big ones. It is not difficult for corporations to 'capture' the CSR process. Inspection of many corporations' environmental reports suggests that comparatively modest gestures are being over-sold, all with the aid of 'environmental auditors' whose existence (and profits) rest on commending the vast majority of environmental and social actions undertaken by corporations. The language of CSR helps – it lends itself easily to rhetorical statements and grandiose claims. This is perhaps a cynical view, but until we have some measure of the actual environmental and social impacts of CSR, it is a view that has to be taken seriously. Moreover, it fits what many see as the continuing primary aim of the shareholders – profits – and the powers they continue to exercise over managements as agents for the achievement of their goals.

Finally, governments are encouraging CSR. Why would they do this? One reason is that governments wish to avoid heavy-handed regulation which they know to be expensive in terms of compliance costs, and hence a risk to employment and economic growth. CSR offers a 'cheap' way of regulating and avoiding the more expensive forms of direct control. The Utilities Act, for example, gives utility regulators the prime duty of looking after consumer interests, but also gives them a secondary duty of caring for environmental and social impacts. The hierarchy suggests that the trade-off between these goals was recognised when the Act was drafted. But compared to having no secondary goals at all, the Act provides an inexpensive if somewhat ambiguous way of securing environmental and social change.

Which of these explanations is the correct one remains to be seen. Maybe some mixture of all of them is an accurate description of what is going on. But one thing is for sure: there are as many, if not more, self-interested reasons why corporations will accede to CSR demands as there are reasons based on some alleged shift in social values away from the corporation as profit-maximiser and towards the corporation as a social enterprise. And if only modest change suffices, the future of the corporation will not look very different from its past. Perhaps the real test will be to see how far CSR survives and flourishes in a recession. Undertaking actions that may involve a sacrifice of profits, albeit a small sacrifice, is comparatively easy when profits are buoyant, but less so when profits are being squeezed. Time will tell.

Notes

1 Professor of Environmental Economics at University College London.

2 W. Hutton, *Putting the 'P' Back into PLC*, The Industrial Society, London, 2001.

3 See Global Reporting Initiative, *Sustainability Reporting Guidelines on Economic and Social Performance*, GRI, Boston, MA, 2000.

4 See *ENDS Report* 294, July 1999, pp. 47–8.

5 European Commission, *Green Paper: Promoting a European Framework for Corporate Social Responsibility*, DC/0/9, Brussels, 2001.

6 David Henderson, *Misguided Virtue: False Notions of Corporate Social Responsibility*, Hobart Paper 142, Institute of Economic Affairs, London, 2001.

5

THE CHANGING ECONOMIC ROLE OF GOVERNMENT

Samuel Brittan[1]

Introduction

At the risk of undermining my own subject, I will stick my neck out and say that the half-century since 1953 has been excessively preoccupied with the economic role of government. We were at all times in danger of forgetting – until rudely awoken by the attack on the New York Twin Towers of 11 September 2001 – that the primary role of government is to look after the physical security of the population, and that all else is secondary.

But even if we confine ourselves to traditional economic variables, the most impressive feature of British growth performance is how stable the underlying trend has been and how little affected by the huffing and puffing of governments. From 1870 until 1950 the best estimate is that UK output per hour grew by 1.25 per cent per annum. From 1950 to 1973 there was a temporary acceleration to 3 per cent. Much of this may have reflected post-war catch-up. In fact this temporary acceleration, so far from being celebrated, was denounced very widely by commentators for not being fast enough compared with Continental and Japanese competitors who were overtaking the UK in some imaginary league table. Since 1973, when governments have become even more preoccupied with boosting productivity, its trend growth rate has fallen back to 2 per cent, and indeed may have been slightly less in the final half of that period.[2]

Productivity is of course not the same as the overall growth rate, which can be affected by variations in 'activity rates' as well as by demographic changes. The slight acceleration in the growth rate predicted in UK government documents for the first decade of the 21st century is due mainly to a faster population growth, itself largely the product of expected *legal* immigration. Although, for such reasons, growth trends have been more variable than productivity ones, even they have still proved pretty stable and resistant to attempts to change them.

Economic policy may thus make much less difference than those who argue about it like to think. That does not mean that we should stop criticising and appraising it. Growth emerges from animal spirits and the human instinct to truck and barter. But it is always possible for policy to have an adverse effect on performance. Sometimes, however, mistaken courses have provoked reactions that have led to their own reversals. For instance, when union power was threatening in the 1970s to make Britain the sick man of Europe there were first the sterling crises of the mid-1970s and then the election of Margaret Thatcher in 1979, both of which produced salutary shocks and associated policy changes.

The 1950s: half-hearted freedom

The year 1953 was a watershed, not only because of the foundation of the Business Economists Group! It was the first year of normality after World War II. The Korean War had come to an end, armaments were at last being run down, and most wartime rationing and control had been lifted. It was also the halfway stage in the somewhat under-discussed post-war Churchill administration of 1951–5. By the time of his stroke in May 1953 Winston Churchill had abandoned his last remaining attempts to establish an overlord system. He himself retreated from the detailed conduct of affairs; and the pygmies took over.

But unfortunately the main chance of a real dash for freedom had already been thrown away. After the Conservatives returned to power a bold scheme to float the pound and free the country from the throes of never-ending runs on sterling had been proposed – 'Operation Robot', named after the two civil servants and one Bank of England official who devised it. The Chancellor, R. A. Butler, was in favour; but Churchill overruled him on the advice of his wartime confidant Lord Cherwell, and the way was open for twenty or more years of preoccupation with sterling and the balance of payments.

Meanwhile so-called league tables began to circulate showing that Continental countries were growing at a faster rate than the UK. The gathering discontent was not a matter of mere numbers. There was a widespread feeling that despite the expansion of educational opportunity and increased prosperity the country was still run in a class-ridden way, and what mattered was not what you knew but whom you knew and possibly how you held your fork. One bestselling book was Michael Shanks's *The Stagnant Society*. Some of these feelings emerged very clearly in John Osborne's play *Look Back in Anger* and in the early novels of Kingsley Amis.

These had their counterpart on the business side. The electrical industry was dominated by three vast bureaucracies. One of them, AEI, was run by Lord Chandos, who gave his real name, Oliver Lyttelton, to part of the National Theatre. A potential interviewer approached him through a series of carpeted rooms, each larger than the other. A journalist knew that if he said or wrote anything that displeased, he might be reported to his editor – or more probably the managing director, whom Chandos was more likely to know socially. Indeed, I was once so reported by a Bank of England director whom I had the temerity to ask for some factual evidence to back the observations he was making 'off the record'. If there is one term which summarises everything against which the reformers were reacting it is 'fuddy-duddyism'.

The decade of growthmanship

There was bound to be some sea change. The reformers were split between those who pinned their hopes on more competition and those who drew their inspiration from French-style indicative planning. Businessmen were just as split as economists or politicians, and probably in an even more muddle-headed way.

The economy did need a competitive shock. The successive rounds of world trade liberalisation had not yet gone far enough to make business anything like an international arena; the vestiges of imperial preference still provided soft external markets; and in many domestic areas restrictive practices abounded.

The reappraisal began well before Harold Wilson formed his Labour government in 1964. There were some earlier acts of liberalisation, such as the abolition of resale price maintenance by Edward Heath. There was also the first attempt at a forward look at public spending, following the Plowden Committee, which reported in the early 1960s. 'Europe' too put in its appearance. Having failed to take part in the negotiations that led to the Treaty of Rome, the Conservative government of Harold Macmillan applied belatedly in 1961 to join the European Union (then called the European Economic Community, and widely known as the 'Common Market') – only to have its application vetoed halfway through negotiations in the famous intervention by General de Gaulle. The latter was much mocked for announcing that Britain was an island; but he was not so far off the mark about the country's psychological unreadiness.

Unfortunately both the planners and the free marketeers had the ground cut from under their feet by the return of sterling and balance of payments crises. The first three years of the Wilson government of 1964–70 were dominated by a futile attempt to prevent sterling devaluation and then, when that failed, by devaluing to another fixed exchange rate. Even after 1967 the Treasury could not divest itself of its balance of payments mentality; and when devaluation seemed slow to work, it threw up a ridiculous contingency plan, 'Operation Brutus', for going back to a wartime siege economy.

Domestically, the government's main form of intervention was devoted to futile attempts at 'prices and incomes policies'. The hope was to keep down costs that way and avoid the need to devalue. Amazingly, neither the Macmillan nor the Wilson governments could see any virtue in stable costs and prices other than in their effect in promoting British exports. There were any number of wage freezes, guiding lights and solemn and binding concordats. Perhaps the worst effect was the attempt to control prices to give the unions an apparent quid pro quo for wage restraint.

The traumas of the 1970s

The surprise return of the Heath government, which was in office from 1970 to 1974, proved in retrospect an interlude in a decade and a half of Labour rule. Most British political commentators regarded a free market approach with horror and raised the spectre of 'Selsdon Man': named after a conference of Conservative leaders before the 1970 election after which the press was briefed in a slightly free market direction. The prime minister, Edward Heath, undoubtedly began with a belief that British industry needed a cold shower. But this was not accompanied by any deeper economic philosophy; and it did not take him long to decide that the road of 'free competition and all that' had been tried and failed and that the required bracing treatment would be applied through yet another attempt at incomes policy.

He was not in fact enthusiastic about statutory wage controls, which he adopted as a fallback after he had failed to reach a voluntary concordat with the trade unions. Ideally he would have liked to have governed by a corporate consensus in which agreements between civil service mandarins and the TUC, rubber-stamped by the CBI, would take the place of normal Cabinet government.

The Heath government did have to cope with an unfortunate legacy. After the 1967 devaluation, inflation did not retreat to its earlier 2 or 3 per cent creeping level, but jumped to 6–7 per cent.

Yet at the same time unemployment was a good deal higher than in the post-war period. In the 1971–2 recession, newspaper headlines celebrated the then horrific total of 'one million unemployed'. The combination of unemployment and inflation, labelled 'stagflation', puzzled economists almost as much as it did politicians. If they had looked beyond their own back yard, they would have seen that the combination of the two evils was far from a rare event – it was normal, for instance, in Latin America, from which they were too proud to draw lessons.

According to the accepted historical canon, it was the miners' strike of early 1974 which brought down the Heath government. But far more significant in fact was an earlier strike in the same industry at the beginning of 1972. The miners' victory then was more significant precisely because it took place in a recession and before there was any thought of a world energy shortage. The economic cards should have been on the government's side. But it was defeated by the violent new tactics of the National Union of Mineworkers, symbolised by the flying pickets, which roamed around the country preventing fuel from being delivered.

After its first defeat by the miners' union, the government moved back towards a dirigiste and supposedly 'expansionist' approach. Despite the inflation figures it began simultaneously to increase government spending and reduce taxes in an attempt to stimulate the economy. Bodies such as the PIB – Prices and Incomes Board – were expected to hold the lid on any inflationary consequences. Although there were some Conservative cynics who welcomed the second miners' strike of 1974 as a vote-winning way of 'bashing the unions', this was far from what Heath wanted. His government blundered into the strike because of wage and price guidelines that made no sense in the context of the new international inflation and because it had completely miscalculated the genuine economic strength of the miners during a world fuel crisis.

The main economic event which affected British business in 1973–4 came from abroad in the shape of a fivefold increase in the price of oil following the Yom Kippur War. The proximate cause was that the Arab-dominated oil-price cartel, OPEC, had at last got its act together. But it was only able to do so because of a simultaneous economic boom in the industrial world, which was reflected to a more moderate extent in the rise of other commodity prices apart from oil.

Until 1971 world inflation has been held at bay by the Bretton Woods dollar standard by which the main industrial countries tied their currencies to the US dollar under a system of 'fixed but adjustable' exchange rates. The emphasis was on the fixed aspect, with adjustment being regarded as a defeatist last resort. The counterpart was that the USA itself acted as the anchor country and maintained reasonably sound money policies.

These were thrown to the wind during the inflationary financing of the Vietnam War in the 1960s. When Congress belatedly enacted a tax increase which failed to stem inflationary forces, political interest was for the first time kindled in the Chicago 'monetarist' school, which advocated domestic monetary control. Even the USA, however, adopted statutory pay and price controls in 1971 just before President Nixon floated the dollar and broke the last links of the US currency with gold. There was one more attempt to fix a new dollar parity; but by 1973 the world was on a floating exchange rate system unconstrained by domestic monetary discipline.

Thus there was nothing to stop the main industrial countries from over-reflating in 1972–3 and indulging in wishful thinking about the rate of economic activity and economic growth that could be sustained without accelerating inflation. A more perfect recipe for the OPEC cartel was hard to imagine. Few countries deliberately sought to inflate their money supply. It was much more that governments such as those of Richard Nixon and Edward Heath – with some support from their central banks – recoiled in horror from the interest rates they thought were necessary to contain the monetary consequences of their own policies. (Germany and Japan were, however, more prepared to give priority to offsetting the inflationary impact of the world oil-price shock than were the English-speaking economies.)

When Labour came back into office, first under Harold Wilson in 1974 and then under James Callaghan in 1976, it inherited an inflation rate racing towards double digits. Its initial response was more of the same: that is, pay and price controls, which they hoped would more easily be accepted under a party that had been created by the union movement. It has to be said that under governments of both persuasions the leaders of British industry proved far too compliant and accepted the wage and price control diagnosis, concentrating mainly on trying to ease the pressure on industry at the margin.

During the whole Labour period of 1974–9, the Chancellor of the Exchequer, Denis Healey, who would have preferred to have been foreign secretary, poured out anathemas on all schools of economic thought. He once declared that he wished to be to economic forecasters what the Boston Strangler was to door-to-door salesmen. He came to share the alarm about the decline of the profitability of British industry and claimed that at tripartite meetings he had to make the case for industry himself. He was also prepared to make some pragmatic gestures towards the control both of public spending and of monetary growth. The monetary controls devised under his regime were, however, too dependent on complicated devices such as the 'corset', which attempted to control bank loans directly and which the shrewder financial practitioners soon found a way round.

The shift away from post-war full employment policies towards a preoccupation with limiting public sector borrowing and a tentative approach to monetary targets was thus apparent during the Labour period. It was dramatised by a series of runs on sterling invariably followed by public expenditure clampdowns, fiercer than anything attempted before or since. The conversion from demand management to a new 'sound money consensus' was often attributed to the conditions imposed by the International Monetary Fund in its 1976 loan negotiations with the UK. In fact government policy had already moved most of the way before the IMF deal was done. The change was symbolised by James Callaghan's speech to the 1976 Labour party conference – widely and correctly attributed to his then son-in-law Peter Jay – in which he declared that governments could no longer spend their way into prosperity.

While world inflation and the accompanying energy price increases of the mid-1970s posed genuine policy dilemmas, the British crisis of the late 1970s was an unnecessary one. Although the UK was well and truly on a floating exchange rate, policy-makers still had the reflexes of a fixed exchange-rate system; and whenever the pound weakened they were afraid that it would do something described in City dining rooms as 'going through the floor'. In retrospect, once appropriate monetary and fiscal policies were introduced the government could have left the pound to recover in its own good time and not bothered with the IMF. Indeed, by 1977 sterling was already recovering too quickly for comfort and British policy-makers experienced the first of a series of strange crises due to an excessively strong pound – 'crises' for which their predecessors would have given a proportion of their anatomy to have. The public sector strikes of early 1979, in which the dead were notoriously left unburied, reflected the boy scout-like desire of the government to use a policy of belt, braces and suspenders against inflation rather than any one or two of these alone.

The advent of Thatcher

Assessment of the Thatcher government is still a matter of acute political controversy which affects even the most highbrow academic attempts to be objective. In retrospect the two main innovations were the belated attack on union power and the privatisation of state-owned industries. The latter was at first regarded as an impossibly utopian project, but was later copied by governments of many different political colours all over the world.

The attack on union power was spearheaded by a number of Acts designed to remove the legal immunities of these bodies and to introduce devices such as strike ballots before industrial action. But other aspects were just as important. The union legislation would not have been so successful had it not been for the government's courageous and successful resistance to yet another miners' strike in 1984–5, one that had unmistakable political motives. But lest too much is attributed to government, one should also draw attention to the secular decline in manufacturing industry – much bemoaned at the time – a sector in which the unions were at their strongest (apart from public employment).

There were also important clearing-up measures. Wage, prices and dividend controls were quickly removed and did not return for the rest of the century. In addition confiscatory marginal tax rates of 80 per cent plus on higher earned incomes and 90 per cent plus on investment income were abolished. The two main tax cuts were in the Geoffrey Howe budget of 1979 and the Nigel Lawson budget of 1988. Although the last led to such an uproar that a House of Commons sitting had to be suspended, there has so far been no attempt by the Blair government to restore these confiscatory rates, whatever may be thought of the overall drift of the tax burden.

What the Thatcher government wished to be remembered for was its total impact in promoting what it called an 'enterprise culture'. It may have had some effect in doing so, judging by business reaction, though there was no productivity acceleration then or later. Indeed, the rhetoric about entrepreneurship was taken up again, in only slightly different words, by Gordon Brown, who became Labour Chancellor in 1997 and who was much influenced by US culture and academic writings, especially of the Harvard variety.

Money and the pound

Unfortunately much of the discussion among economists and economic commentators during the Thatcher period was on pseudo-technical questions of monetary control. The dilemma started from the very beginning in 1979–80, when the official broad measure of the money supply, sterling M3,[3] was rising much faster than target; but this apparent monetary expansion was accompanied by a severe recession and a further rise in the pound about which British exporters complained bitterly. The renewed upward pressure on sterling was widely attributed to the impact of North Sea oil, which was then just coming on-stream, on the British balance of payments. One industrialist remarked that he wished that the 'bloody stuff' had been left under the ground.

A more highbrow reaction to the rising pound was to argue that the British government had used the wrong measure on the money supply and should have used some narrower aggregate. This view seemed to be adopted in 1984–5, when, to the fury of another school of monetarists, the government abandoned targets for sterling M3 and moved over to a very narrow money aggregate called M0. This consisted of the banks' balances with the Bank of England together with cash in the hands of the public. This aggregate was not, however, used as a form of monetary base control, for which the Friedmanites[4] had argued, but as a rough guide to current economic conditions. The truth is that the government did not find any monetary indicator that conformed to common-sense observation of what was happening to the economy.

One effect of all this squabbling was to put the general public – and even non-specialist economists – off anything to do with monetarism. Another effect was to build support for British membership of the European Monetary System, which had started without the UK in 1979. It was noted that some countries, notably France, had managed to import German price stability by tying their currencies to the German mark inside the European Exchange Rate Mechanism and realigning as little and as seldom as possible. The clamour to join the ERM was shared by far more people than chose to remember it afterwards.

There were two forms of the argument for a 'D-mark anchor'. One was that the UK would have to follow a non-inflationary monetary policy if it was to avoid realignment; and the movement of the sterling market exchange rate would therefore send forth the right signals. Another argument was that the pressure of overseas competition, without the devaluation option, would put a lid on British costs and prices in international markets, and this would eventually percolate through to the domestic economy as well. Whether the external discipline and monetary control arguments were complementary or alternative, or amounted to the same thing, would take a lifetime of scholastic argument to determine. Business support for the ERM was based more simply on the hope of some exchange-rate stability that would make life easier.

The case for the ERM as a monetary anchor was probably at its strongest in 1985 when the Chancellor, Nigel Lawson, first proposed it. Although it had a large amount of Cabinet support, it was vetoed by Margaret Thatcher, who was by then relying increasingly on the advice of her own personal economic adviser, Alan Walters, much of it given from across the Atlantic. There was another attempt at a more informal link with the ERM through the policy of shadowing the Deutschmark, which Lawson adopted in 1987 and which led to a much-publicised row with the prime minister in 1988 – a dispute culminating in the Chancellor's resignation in the following year.

The third attempt on the ERM was that of John Major, who succeeded Lawson as Chancellor and who managed to force through British membership in the autumn of 1990. By then the Treasury had no alternative policy to offer, and Margaret Thatcher resigned near the end of that year after a disappointing leadership vote among Conservative MPs. But by then the case for the Deutschmark anchor had been enormously weakened by the German reunification of 1989, which imposed a large budgetary burden on the German government. The Bundesbank, quite rightly in view of its mandate, maintained high interest rates to offset the inflationary effects. This interest rate policy was, however, quite unsuitable for the UK, which had entered one of its worst post-war recessions, one particularly resented because it hit the talking classes in the south east of England. Thus by 1992 John

Major, who was by then prime minister, was forced to take Britain out of the ERM and put the country back on a floating exchange rate, which lasted for the rest of the 1990s and into the next century.

The more stable 1990s

The decade from 1992 witnessed first a gradual recovery from the recession and then a period of low inflation and moderate growth, with more stability than had been seen for many years past. The hallmarks of the new policies were inflation targets and a greater role for the Bank of England.

Probably the pioneering country in the use of inflation targets was New Zealand. But someone in the Treasury had the sense to propose them for the UK as part of the response to the post-ERM panic. These targets were accompanied by a new obligation on the part of the Bank of England to produce a regular Inflation Report. These innovations, introduced by Norman Lamont, who had succeeded Major as Chancellor, were reinforced when his successor Kenneth Clarke surprised many officials by agreeing to the publication of the minutes of the monthly meetings on interest rate policy between the Chancellor and the Governor of the Bank of England.

'Operational independence' of the Bank came with the Labour victory of 1997. It had first been advocated by Nigel Lawson and then by Norman Lamont, but proved unacceptable to both Thatcher and Major. Tony Blair, who had no ambition to control monetary policy personally, was more easily persuaded. The new policy regime, under which interest rates were set by a nine-person Monetary Policy Committee, was more of an evolution than the revolution that Gordon Brown's supporters liked to claim.

The most interesting feature of the 1990s was not so much low and stable inflation itself, but the fact that it was accompanied by a continuing drop in unemployment to much lower levels than in the 1980s. In economic jargon, the NAIRU – the rate of unemployment consistent with non-accelerating inflation – seemed to have dropped. Some of the credit can legitimately be granted to the Labour 'New Deal', which put emphasis on retraining and on pressure on the unemployed to take jobs and temporary subsidies to employers to take them on. Even more important in my view was the belated effect of the reduction of union power to price people out of work arising from the Thatcher measures of the 1980s.

Labour leaders could not of course publicly admit this. But privately they were keen to emphasise how little of the Conservative union legislation they had reversed. Nevertheless there was some quiet backsliding. The minimum wage was more objectionable to libertarians in principle than in practice, as the government was keen to keep it low, to the chagrin of its own left wing. Nevertheless there was a creeping movement back towards so-called 'social' legislation, which imposed high cost obligations on employers. (At the time of writing British employers are up in arms against a draft EU directive that grants all temporary workers the same conditions and terms as their permanent colleagues – thus closing one route for pricing workers into jobs. The British government was mainly concerned to delay this rule for the first six weeks rather than to stop it altogether.)

There were a great many specific domestic measures that ministers undoubtedly believed were improving the supply side and making the economy more competitive; and it is true that most of them had been sanctioned by official economists as ways of tackling one or other 'externality' that interfered with the optimal working of the market mechanism. But what the new government found it difficult to appreciate was that the cumulative effect of a great many individual measures, which in themselves might have been desirable, produced an irritating and cost-increasing business environment. Unfortunately the new government's academic praetorian guard was not as familiar with the US economic analysis of government failure as it was with the standard writing on 'market failure'.

The argument about Europe rumbled on, threatening to split the Labour Party as it already had the Conservatives. The economic argument no longer related to an exchange-rate anchor. Many supporters of British membership of the euro had originally seen it as the best way to establish an independent central bank. But with the coming of the MPC arrangement, this argument had largely vanished. What was at stake now were the pros and cons of a more stable exchange rate against the disadvantages of a 'one size fits all' monetary policy. Or to put it another way: would stability be better ensured by the MPC or the European Central Bank? No amount of technical analysis was likely to weaken the conclusion that it was half a dozen of one and six of the other. The famous five economic tests for euro membership could be interpreted according to taste and their application was delayed as long as possible.

In any case public opinion remained for long resolutely opposed to dropping the pound; and Tony Blair would have been well advised to put the whole issue on ice for his first two administrations. His reluctance to do so had little to do with euro technicalities and reflected far more the urgings of Foreign Office and Cabinet Office officials who wanted Britain to have a seat at some imaginary European top table.

Conclusion: the new century

As the new century began there was a distinct possibility of old errors coming back in a new way. The most likely route was by means of the European Social Model, which was not social, not a model and did not deserve the name European. It was characterised by high labour overheads, wage arrangements that made it difficult to fire – and therefore to hire – and which were too insensitive to market pressures.

The result was that an excessively low proportion of the EU population was at work, especially in the older age groups; and the coming explosion in the number of pensioners looked like having to be supported by an ever lower proportion of active workers. Too many people were 'being educated', unemployed or prematurely retired. The simple step of linking retirement age with longevity, which might at least have eased the pressure on the European welfare state, was considered too revolutionary, and reformers became obsessed with the minutiae of pensions arrangements.

The UK debate was muddled by an unhelpful dispute between the Little Englanders and the euro enthusiasts. Yet for those of us who treated government as a device rather than a totem, it did not matter so much exactly where the centre of power was located. The British economy was equally capable of flourishing under a strong European federal government with appropriate decentralisation and a single currency, or under a national government with an independent pound regulated by the Bank of England Monetary Policy Committee. The danger was that it would get the worst of both worlds: a weak European confederation, with enough power to stifle market forces and price people out of work, but without the power or drive for genuine reform.

Yet, for all these problems, most British people had a far higher standard of living than the vast majority of the human race in all past history; and the time could be coming for Lord Keynes's 'Economic Possibilities for our Grandchildren', in which attention would shift to more important matters. That is if the attempts of religious and other fundamentalists to destroy the European Enlightenment and the appeasing reaction of Europe's leaders do not derail us on the way.

Notes

1   *Financial Times* columnist.
2   N. F. R. Crafts, *Britain's Relative Economic Decline*, Institute of Economic Affairs, 2002.
3   See Note 4, Chapter 6 – *Ed.*
4   See Chapters 6 and 8 – *Ed.*

6

MONEY AND MONETARY POLICY

C. A. E. Goodhart [1]

Some history

The UK came out of World War II heavily burdened with government debt, owed both internally and externally, and with a comprehensive system of direct controls to restrain demand, including controls over credit extension by banks and new capital issues, as well as exchange controls over international capital flows. For a variety of reasons the UK was slower to abandon such direct financial controls than most of our competitors, including those western European countries whose economies had suffered more physically.

Partly in order to facilitate the continued conduct of such direct controls, the various financial institutions, notably the banks, were encouraged to form themselves into clubs, and to confine their lending activities to certain restricted areas. Thus the building societies offered personal sector mortgages, and nothing else, and no one else did so; the finance houses were the sole providers of consumer credit, the banks usually being discouraged from making loans to persons; and so on. In other words the financial system was heavily cartelised, with official approval. With competition being so limited, spreads were set so as to generate comfortable profits, with not much risk. In some ways the major players in the UK's financial system, the clearing banks, became administrative extensions of HM Treasury, whose main function was to say 'no' to prospective borrowers who had been classified as less worthy by the government – in rising order of unworthiness, entrepreneurs in service industries, persons, importers.

Of course, such constraints on free competition led to losses of efficiency, both static and dynamic. How much the continuing inefficiencies in our domestic financial system led to the UK growing more slowly than its main competitors would be difficult to assess. That said, the early decades after 1945, until the 1970s, displayed a faster rate of growth than at any other time in our history, so the restrictive financial regime cannot have had *too* adverse an effect.

Besides the legacy of wartime controls, post-war governments, in reaction against the experiences of the 1930s, believed in the need to manage domestic demand to avoid unemployment – and, following the ideas developed by Keynes, in the possibility of doing so. The main instruments for managing demand were seen to be, in order of importance, fiscal policy first, direct credit controls second, and interest rates last. However, while revisions to direct credit ceilings were a major, perhaps the main, feature of official contra-cyclical measures in the financial arena in the 1950s and 1960s, it is difficult to control excessive upward pressures on expenditures by direct measures alone. Money is fungible, so officially favoured firms with access to credit could lend on to less favoured firms via trade credit; internationally firms could avoid exchange controls via the dreaded 'leads and lags'; new financial institutions could develop, for example the 'fringe banks', whose *raison d'être* was largely that they were not subject to the same controls as the established banks.

Partly in consequence, partly because of an appreciation of the merits of free markets, the authorities in the UK began, with the initiative coming from the Conservatives when in office, but accepted albeit somewhat grudgingly by Labour governments, to put more weight on the price mechanism in the guise of official changes in Bank rate. At this time academic studies in the UK of the responses of businessmen and consumers to interest rate changes indicated that expenditure would be interest inelastic. However, interest rates had a comparative advantage on the external front in that they also influenced international monetary and capital flows. So the main factor causing spike increases in interest rates was usually pressures on the exchange rate, which was pegged to the US dollar under the Bretton Woods system. In general, however, with the government remaining a large debtor, with lobbying pressures from other debtors, for example business and house owners with mortgages, and monetary policy seen anyhow as a weak reed (recall the Radcliffe Report in 1959),[2] nominal and real interest rates were held quite low, except under the influence of external crises. Following the constitutional changes arising from the two world wars and the inter-war slump, interest rate decisions were in the hands of the Chancellor; the Bank of England saw itself primarily as a behind-the-scenes adviser, and the Treasury was only too happy to keep the Bank out of the limelight.

Meanwhile, with interest rates officially set and rate differentials largely fixed, the banks were naturally able and happy to accept whatever funds were deposited with them. Whenever the growth of bank lending rose at a faster rate than their deposit base permitted, they ran off their government debt. This allowed the supply of money to adjust to the demand for money, itself a stable function of incomes and interest rates. That self-same stability in the demand for money function had been earlier found in the USA, and formed the main pillar of the new doctrine of monetarism, emerging from Chicago and Milton Friedman. Given that the demand for money was a predictable function of incomes and interest rates, and that prices/wages were sufficiently flexible (unless subjected to extreme and unpredictable shocks) to restore the economy to full employment, then appropriate control over monetary growth would deliver price stability. Inflation was a monetary phenomenon. This was heresy to British Keynesians. Monetary velocity was thought to be highly variable (the Radcliffe Report again), monetary policy of limited efficiency, and inflation largely a function of 'wage push' and hence amenable to incomes policies.

Although the main driving force for the 'Competition and Credit Control' (CCC) reform of 1971 was a desire, by the Bank mainly, to be rid of direct credit controls (in the context of an eventually successful recovery from the 1967 devaluation), the finding of stable demand for money functions in the UK up till then did provide support, because it suggested that overall monetary, and credit, control could be achieved by acceptable variations in interest rates. In the event, CCC coincided with a major world boom, and the commercial banks were keen to exert their new competitive position to expand their customer base. Bank lending rose extremely sharply in 1972–3, and the banks funded this through liability management, effectively raising yields on Certificates of Deposit[3] and other wholesale liabilities relative to other rates. This caused interest differentials to shift in a way never previously experienced; as a result the growth in broad money, as measured by sterling M3 (£M3),[4] was much faster than was consistent with the previous demand for money functions. Meanwhile the commodity price rise, and then the subsequent oil-price hike, brought about an adverse supply shock. The Conservative government retreated to an incomes policy. Although nominal interest rates were increased (to 13 per cent), they remained well below both the actual and expected rate of inflation; a revised version of direct credit controls was reintroduced – the 'corset' – which remained, on and off, until 1981.

After the introduction of the corset, £M3 grew more slowly, while inflation rose rapidly, so that the normal relativities between £M3, nominal incomes and interest rates were restored in 1975. This convinced the new Conservative leadership, now in opposition, that the surge in £M3 was a monetary shock that had led to the subsequent inflation. Germany had by now moved to monetary targeting, and this was becoming internationally fashionable. When the UK sought financial assistance from the IMF in the crisis of 1976, it too began to flirt with monetary targeting, albeit with many left-wing Keynesian reservations.

Such hesitations were, naturally, cast aside when the Conservatives regained power in 1979; a target for £M3 was made the centrepiece of the new Medium Term Financial Strategy. Again the context was not auspicious. A second oil shock, combined with an indirect tax hike, and large public sector wage payments led to a spike in inflation, which was not accommodated by the optimistically low monetary target. Shortly thereafter the removal of the corset resulted in a (temporary) blow-out of monetary growth, well in excess of the new target.

At the same time a combination of a sharply appreciating real exchange rate, a restrictive budget and quite high nominal interest rates was leading to a sharp, but quite short-lived, drop in output in 1981–2, and to a decline in inflation at least as fast as had ever been intended or desired. Despite the target overshoot, the appearance was of tight (not easy) monetary policy. Moreover Alan Walters, Mrs Thatcher's new adviser, and his colleague, the monetary economist Niehans, had doubts as to whether £M3 was *the* correct measure of 'money'. Perhaps a narrower version, M1 or M0, or a yet broader version, M4 or M5, including building society deposits, was somehow superior, or even some theoretical (Divisia) index weighting of all the Ms. And narrow money, M1, was growing much more slowly.

Also at the start of the 1980s, a number of new structural innovations were appearing, here and in the USA, such as interest-bearing sight deposits, money-market mutual funds, offshore euro deposits, etc., etc. Almost all the demand for money functions, and usually those used domestically as targets, began to misbehave. As Governor Bouey of the Bank of Canada is supposed to have remarked, 'We did not abandon the monetary targets; they abandoned us.' In the UK, as in the USA and Canada (but not in Germany), from about 1983 onwards opinion shifted from the view that velocity was predictable and monetary targets central to policy, to the view that velocity was too unpredictable and monetary targets effectively useless, or worse.

But that removed the 'anchor' by which monetary policy was supposed to be controlled, and price stability assured. There followed a remarkable period of policy-making wherein the

Chancellor, Nigel Lawson, sought to make membership of the European Exchange Rate Mechanism an external anchor for monetary policy, while at the same time rejecting claims that moves towards monetary union in Europe had political, i.e. federal, implications. Mrs Thatcher saw that they did have such implications, and opposed the move, at least until splits in her government and conjunctural economic arguments persuaded her that it was a tactically correct move, and we joined the ERM in October 1990.

Because of the economically botched nature of Germany's reunion, the Bundesbank had to keep interest rates high in 1991–2, despite a deepening depression in much of the rest of Europe. Political divisions in the Conservative Party about the ERM, and the European Union more generally, meant that there was no willingness in the UK to tighten monetary policy for the sole purpose of protecting our ERM parity. So when speculation arose, for a variety of reasons, about the future of European exchange-rate regimes, the UK was a 'sitting duck' and was duly shot out of the system in September 1992.

The present monetary regime

That forced exit led to a rethink which ushered in the UK's present regime. One of the enduring legacies of economics theory from the 1960s and 1970s was the view that in the medium and longer term there was no trade-off between inflation and real variables, such as output growth and unemployment – i.e. that in the long term the Phillips curve[5] is vertical. Over such a longer horizon real variables would be essentially determined by real factors, though really bad monetary policy causing hyperinflation or deflation could have a long-term deleterious effect. If so, then the primary objective of monetary policy, and the best way to support sustainable growth, would be to aim policy at achieving a low and stable inflation rate. Moreover, the pessimism as to whether interest rates could affect expenditures, which had been prevalent in the UK in the 1950s and 1960s, had been replaced by confidence that interest rate adjustments, via changes in the official short-term rate, could be effective in controlling nominal incomes and expenditures. Indeed, that confidence has since been enhanced in the USA and the UK by the apparently adroit way in which monetary policy was managed in the 1990s to maintain steady growth; whereas the failure of the zero interest rate policy in Japan to restore growth has been categorised as being a result of policy errors, rather than of intrinsic weakness in the monetary instruments themselves.

So, in accord with both theory and growing fashion around the world in the design of monetary policy, the new regime, introduced in 1992–3 by the Chancellor, Norman Lamont, was one of direct inflation targets, with variations in interest rates being the operational instrument. But there was a catch. Whatever the monetary regime, Chancellors and prime ministers had always promised to achieve price stability. But when the time came to raise interest rates to achieve that promise, generally a politically unpopular step which reduces demand and raises unemployment, ministers would hesitate, often citing the unreliability of the forecasts and the desirability of deferring unpopular measures until the need for them was clearer. This resulted in policy measures being, or at least perceived as being, systematically 'too little, too late'. An elegant theoretical construct, termed 'time inconsistency', was developed in support of this, and myriad academic articles written.

Anyhow, the bottom line was that people did not trust the politicians to take the steps needed to hit an inflation target. The solution that was found for this was to delegate the task of achieving price stability to an operationally independent central bank, although the exact definition of price stability was often set by the government, as in the UK, or agreed between government and central bank, as in New Zealand. With a single, publicly known quantitative target, and one instrument to achieve that, the operationally independent central bank can, and should, be both transparent and accountable. Indeed, monetary policy is now more transparent and accountable than in any other previous regime, with the possible exception of the pre-1914 gold standard.

Politicians rarely cede levers of power and influence without a fight. Prime Minister Major was unprepared to do so during his years in office, 1992–7, so Chancellor Lamont moved in cautious steps towards granting more independence to the Bank, and Chancellor Clarke was even more persuaded of his own comparative advantage in setting interest rates. Nevertheless, the inflation target was reinforced by encouraging the Bank to write and publish its independent Inflation Forecast, reversing previous Treasury censorship of published Bank papers, and thereby giving an authoritative but independent picture of the likely course of future inflation. Although the final decision on interest rates remained with the Chancellor, the monthly policy discussion between the Chancellor and Governor was published (the Ken [Clarke] and Eddie [George] show); the Governor's opening statement was read into the minutes verbatim; and the Bank was allowed to decide on the exact timing over the next week, or so, of any change in interest rates.

Nevertheless, such changes, apart from the quarterly publication of the Inflation Report, were quite minor compared with the regime change introduced by Chancellor Gordon Brown on taking office in May 1997. He gave the Bank, in the guise of its newly constructed Monetary Policy Committee (MPC), with five internal Bank members and four external appointed members, operational independence to set interest rates for the purpose of hitting an inflation target, set by the Chancellor. This was set, and has remained, as +2.5 per cent per annum measured by the 'RPIX'[6] over an indefinite period. This sudden regime change had not been foreshadowed, for example in the Labour Party's manifesto, which instead talked about testing the quality of the Bank's advice over a lengthy period; so there is little documentation yet of the precise rationale, as viewed by its progenitors, either for the regime change overall, or for the component elements of the structure – for example, of the need for the MPC to write a letter of explanation to the Chancellor should RPIX fall outside a band of 1 per cent either side of the target. On the other hand the general argumentation in favour of granting a central bank operational independence was well understood by the mid-1990s; its adoption by the UK came midway among a lengthy series of central banks around the world doing the same.

Compared with the record of previous fluctuations in inflation, a 1 per cent band on either side of the point target seemed minuscule, and Bank Deputy Governor King joked that 'this would revive the lost English art of letter writing'. In the event, however, as of the date of writing (February 2003), no such letters have had to be written, and the rate of both inflation, around its 2.5 per cent target, and of output growth, around its 'equilibrium' trend, have remained extraordinarily stable, despite numerous shocks elsewhere, for example the Asian crisis in 1997–8 and the 'tech' bubble and bust between 1999 and 2002. The new monetary regime, and its conduct, must take some, though probably not all, of the credit for that.

With interest rates being set directly, by the MPC, to aim to control the final objective of price stability, what role, if any, remains for the monetary aggregates, for example as intermediate information variables, in the policy domain? The answer is 'not a lot'; though the range of opinion varies between those who give considerable lip-service to monetary growth (in the Bundesbank and ECB), but who rarely base policy decisions on it, to those, in the more Anglo-Saxon central banks, who regard discussions of these aggregates as largely a waste of time. Nevertheless, such data can provide useful additional information both on conditions in key credit markets, and on the demand and supply of liquidity in the main sectors of the economy. There are circumstances, for example of credit crunches, of financial instability, and where interest rates are constrained by the zero lower bound, to name but a selection, where the monetary data can be informationally most useful. Nevertheless, monetary developments have been, and are continuing to be, subject to structural changes. These have caused sharp, and unpredicted, changes in velocity in the past, which can cloud the interpretation of developments in the monetary aggregates.

The future of monetary policy

Indeed, the enthusiasm, and hype, surrounding the 'new economy' and its information technology led to dramatic scenarios of what might happen to payments systems, to financial institutions and to money itself, even leading some to query whether current central bank control mechanisms could last for long. In particular there is no doubt that electronic payment mechanisms are much cheaper than paper-based chequeing systems; despite the sizeable cross-subsidy given to cheque-based payments, they are, and will be, increasingly phased out and replaced by electronic payments.

This led some to query whether paper (or now plastic) cash would also be replaced by electronic payment vehicles, debit or credit cards of differing degrees of 'smartness'. In practice cards have little economic advantage, in cost or ease of transactions, at the petty cash level for small purchases. Moreover the bulk of cash holdings by value is held in large notes whose great advantage, at least for the foreseeable future, lies in their anonymity; cash is much less easily traced than electronic transfers. So it is the store of value and means of payment of choice of those trying to avoid or to evade the law in the grey and black economies. More generally, smart electronic devices, in payment mechanisms as elsewhere, hold out the prospects of monitoring, even in real time, exactly what payments the holder is making; this raises the general issue of privacy versus efficiency, which will be a continuing battle area over coming decades.

If cash were to disappear (which in practice it will not do), or were to be phased out in order to enhance greater centralised economic control, much of the monetary base, the liabilities of the central banks, would also go. This has raised in some quarters a concern as to whether the central bank could still make its official interest rate effective. But the authorities, if they so want, can always rig the system so that the main financial institutions have to hold, and large value payments are settled in, central bank liabilities. Theoretical studies of cashless systems suggest that central bank control over short-term nominal interest rates does not appear threatened by any current or foreseeable technological developments.

What is more uncertain is whether the traditional arrangement whereby each sovereign state has its own separate currency may now shift. In the new global system in which goods and capital, but *not* labour, can move quickly and at little cost between borders, but in which floating exchange rates appear, for reasons not well understood, to vary in a disorderly fashion, there are now serious questions as to whether it is better for relatively small open economies to maintain their own separate currencies, or simply adopt a common currency with its larger trading partners. The eurozone has led the way, but one could envisage most of the Americas becoming a dollar zone, and Africa and the Middle East part of the eurozone. In this context one must add that the question of interaction between a wider, possibly federal, monetary area and independent fiscal policies in the constituent nation states has not yet been worked out (the Amsterdam Stability and Growth Pact is an initial, and imperfect, cock-shy at it); this could still blow the concept of wider currency areas out of the water.

Even if cash, the role of the central bank and, perhaps, the link between the nation state and its separate currency remain intact over the next few decades, the role and balance sheet structure of financial intermediaries are likely to show considerable change in coming years. One of the features of modern financial technology is that it allows the various elements in a financial operation, such as making a loan, to be unbundled and organised separately – for example, origination, funding, bearing the interest rate and credit risks. Securitisation, transferring debt off the books of the origi-nating institution, is perhaps the best-known new technique.

Various forms of swaps and derivatives, notably credit derivatives, are also important in allowing idiosyncratic risk to be diversified away, and common risks to be transferred to those willing to absorb them.

Such possibilities for attaining greater specialisation of function might be accompanied by greater specialisation in form among financial intermediaries. In the last couple of decades the trend has all been in the opposite direction, with the increasing dominance of the universal bank incorporating the functions not only of a commercial bank and an investment bank, but also those of an insurance company, a fund manager and a research team. Moreover the growth of multinational universal banks has mimicked that of multinational industrial and commercial firms; so much so that some pundits have averred that banking would be dominated by not more than about ten multinational monster banks within the decade. I have my doubts. The greater ease of specialisation, through the use of sophisticated market transactions, combined with the various disadvantages of the multinational universal bank – for example, managerial complications and internal conflicts of interest – could see the recent trends towards size and universal functional form reverse, but that is a hazardous prediction.

Be that as it may, the definition of a bank whose liability (a deposit) counts as money, since it can be used as, or rapidly transformed into, a means of payment, is going to come under increasing stress. Financial institutions, such as unit trusts or mortgage institutions, will increasingly be prepared to liquefy, i.e. to grant immediate access to payment facilities, against any assets held by persons, real or financial. Even in the absence of assets, a wide range of financial institutions will be prepared to provide instant credit, for the time being via plastic cards, against a borrower's future income. In this context, in which prior liquidity constraints are almost totally removed, there will be a need for increased attention to the design of personal bankruptcy legislation, and of how to protect short-sighted and credulous individuals from themselves.

At the same time the range of financial assets available for individuals to buy is likely to expand. The huge, and not repeatable, bull market in equities in the 1990s focused everyone's attention on the stock market. At a time when it seemed that investors might reasonably expect yields of 20 per cent per annum on equities into the distant future, 'the wild blue yonder', who cares about designing anything else? The stock market collapse of the early 2000s reminded investors that not only would real profits and earnings grow only on average in line with the real economy, at, say, 2–3.5 per cent per annum, but also that much of such earnings would be creamed off by the company managers themselves, and by other insiders. Attempts to make managers work for the shareholders, rather than primarily just for themselves, will be tried, but are likely to fail.

The cult of the equity will take something of a beating. If central banks can make operational independence work well enough to maintain price stability, and thus expectations of price stability, intact over coming decades, traditional bonds may come back into favour, but they are hardly a glamorous savings instrument. In this context there may well be a proliferation of new types of assets, conditioned in a variety of ways on a variety of economic, and personal, outcomes.

Certainly many changes in the form of financial institutions, financial markets and financial assets can be expected in the next few decades, including very likely the ambit and definition of money. But, as of this moment, my expectation is that the role and function of the central bank as the institution that determines the level of the official short-term nominal interest rate is likely to be one of the most enduring elements among the flux of the future. But what bodies will regulate the financial system, and what form such regulation may take, is a far murkier issue, where my glass ball with its view of the future remains resolutely opaque.

Notes

1   Until recently held the Norman Sosnow Chair of Banking and Finance at the London School of Economics, and earlier was one of the first external members of the Bank of England's Monetary Policy Committee.

2   *Report of the Committee on the Working of the Monetary System* (Cmnd. 827), HMSO, London, 1959.

3   Certificates of Deposit (CDs) are tradable instruments, as contrasted with ordinary deposits which are not. CDs give the holder a claim for a stated sum of money from the issuing bank on a stated day.

4   Sterling M3 is a broad definition of the money supply, comprising all sterling monetary deposits (plus currency) held by UK residents in banks in the UK.

5   The 'Phillips curve', relating the rate of inflation to the rate of unemployment, was initially researched by Professor Bill Phillips of the London School of Economics. See A. W. H. Phillips, *Collected Works in Contemporary Perspective*, Cambridge University Press, 2000.

6   The Retail Price Index excluding the direct effect of interest rate changes.

7

COUNTING THE CANDLE-ENDS: FISCAL POLICY SINCE WORLD WAR II

Richard Holt[1]

Over the last half-century, few topics have received as much attention from economists as have the theory and practice of fiscal policy. This mirrors a similar preoccupation on the part of politicians, and of those who write and talk about politics. The annual Budget is at least as significant an event in the British political calendar as the Queen's Speech; and the financial constraints that the Treasury places upon all other government departments and agencies are a constant source of complaint and public disapproval. In matters of public finance the Chancellor dominates all but one of his colleagues, and by doing so he dominates much of the government's wider political agenda.[2]

It was not always so. Hugh Dalton, Britain's first post-war Chancellor, was famously disappointed not to have been offered the Foreign Office. For Dalton the business of adding up the public spending and revenue totals and worrying over the difference between the two seemed likely to be a poor second to that of creating a new world moral and political order. And that was despite the fact that Dalton was not only an economist by profession, but one who had written a widely respected textbook on public finances, and who had a strong interest in the scope for using taxes to redistribute income and wealth within society. If anybody was likely to be keen on the job of Chancellor, and its fiscal duties, then surely it should have been Hugh Dalton.

The post of Chancellor turned out to be far more challenging than Dalton had expected, partly because his authority as Chancellor was not at all accepted within Cabinet. Initially Dalton was able to take delight in providing the funds for the creation of the welfare state, but he became increasingly indignant at the assumption of other ministers that his task was simply to provide the cash for their spending plans, irrespective of the nation's ability to afford those plans. Since Dalton had a low opinion of most of his colleagues, and also a tendency to make all his opinions well known, there was widespread relief when, in 1947, Dalton resigned from the Treasury following a leak of Budget secrets.

In the context of the time, the affordability that bothered Dalton was largely to do with access to foreign capital, and with the chronic problems that then existed with the nation's external balance of payments. Anything that boosted domestic demand was problematic in an economy that was hugely dependent on overseas trade, which was deeply war damaged and uncompetitive, and which was operating within an international economic order that made too little allowance for the problems of post-war transition. Dalton, however, struggled to articulate his problem in quite that way, since he was also reluctant to accept the intellectual framework offered to him by his former teacher turned adviser, the annoyingly brilliant and exotic Maynard Keynes. Dalton believed that the way to run an economy was through the management of supply (involving rationing, price controls, production quotas, import barriers, and the like – though none of these was actually his responsibility as Chancellor); Keynes argued that it was the management of demand which mattered, and that the fiscal balance was the instrument of choice for achieving rational demand management.[3]

By the time Stafford Cripps succeeded Hugh Dalton as Chancellor, the Treasury had largely come round to the Keynesian view, and it took the new Chancellor along with it.[4] Cripps was the first Chancellor to frame the annual Budget in terms of its impact on demand in the economy, something that earned him the sobriquet of 'the first modern Chancellor'.[5] For the next 30 years Keynesian demand management would be the explicit and central organising idea of British economic policy-making – or to be more precise it would be the explicit and central *set of organising and even disorganising ideas*, some of them inconsistent with one another, and many of them inconsistent with what Keynes himself had said and meant, and with underlying economic theory and common sense alike.

In the mid- to late 1970s the paradigm appeared to shift. The reasons for this are well known: unemployment and inflation were rising in tandem rather than being the offsetting phenomena it had previously been thought they were; and it looked as if the growth of the state sector was acting to suppress the underlying growth rate of the economy, essentially by rewarding inefficiency and by penalising achievement. As a result, Denis Healey became in effect the 'last modern Chancellor' when in 1976 his prime minister, Jim Callaghan, announced that the nation could no longer spend its way out of recession – if it ever could. Callaghan's words were written for him by the economics editor of *The Times*, who happened to be his son-in-law: the best of all evidence of how Establishment thinking had changed.

Except that, of course, there is always continuity as well as change. The tax rises and spending cuts that Healey imposed in 1976 were little different to those that Callaghan himself had imposed a decade earlier, and indeed little different to the policies of Stafford Cripps, who was not known as 'austerity Cripps' for nothing. Furthermore, Healey's successor, Geoffrey Howe, may have told people that he was a monetarist and not a Keynesian, but what he really did was impose very austere fiscal policies on the economy, while quickly giving up on the largely fantastic notion of controlling monetary growth. So rhetoric changed hugely in the late 1970s, but practical policies changed less so.

Meanwhile the real hard-core economic theorists embarked on

a rather different and even more fantastical journey of their own.

At the time the prevailing Keynesian view was that an increase or decrease in government borrowing might be expected to raise or lower demand and hence output in the economy. But in 1974 the American economist Robert Barro published an article in the *Journal of Political Economy* in which he questioned that view.[6] Barro argued that an increase in government spending funded by borrowing, in the form of the issue of government debt, has a similar impact on demand as an increase that is funded by higher taxes – i.e. very little.[7] This is because the bonds need to be repaid, thereby creating a *future* taxation burden that is much the same as the increase that is being avoided in the *current* tax burden. That in turn implies that fiscal fine-tuning is unlikely to work: the increase in government spending will be met by a rise in private sector saving, as households and companies put income aside to cover future increases in their tax bills.

Barro's theory was not really new: indeed, it originated with the great eighteenth-century Scottish economist David Ricardo, and it went by the rather fancy name of 'Ricardian equivalence'. What Barro did was to tidy up some mistakes in other people's formulations to make the theory robust.

Just as Ricardian equivalence says that fiscal policy cannot be used to stimulate the economy, so it also implies that, when a government finds itself in a recession but with a large fiscal deficit, it can cheerfully raise taxes to reduce the deficit since the higher taxes will not reduce demand.[8]

Results such as these might be regarded as giving support to some of the more controversial fiscal policies of the Conservative Chancellors of the Thatcher/Major years, such as the 1981 and 1993 Budgets of Geoffrey Howe and Norman Lamont respectively, which raised taxes during recessions. By the same token, Ricardian equivalence might also be said to support Nigel Lawson's 1988 Budget, which cut taxes during a boom, as well as supporting the Conservative governments' more generalised suspicion of fine-tuning.

However, an alternative view of government borrowing is that it is in part a rather clever mechanism whereby the government helps the private sector to transfer some of its future spending power into the present. And that may well be a sensible thing for a government to do, if future incomes are going to be higher than current ones, either because the economy is in a temporary recession, or because there is positive underlying economic growth. Indeed, if the government's purpose is to invest in physical or intellectual capital, with the aim of generating the economic growth itself, then borrowing to fund that investment looks an especially sensible thing to do.

There is a problem here, which is that the 'rather clever mechanism' may be cleverer in theory than in practice, since the public sector may not be very wise in the way in which it spends the cash that it raises. This is an important issue, and one that was used with considerable justification by Conservative ministers from 1979 onwards to defend cuts in taxes, and in government spending plans. The current Labour administration shares the scepticism, but has responded differently: it has sought to develop a system of performance targets that it believes will raise the quality of government spending. That system has been controversial to say the least, and the kindest thing to say is that the new approach has not yet fully proved itself.

However, advocates of Ricardian equivalence have a more basic, and to them more convincing, way of defending their view of the world. They say that there is no need for the public sector to borrow from the future on behalf of the private sector, since the private sector can itself always borrow against its future, higher, income. That is indeed what Barro assumed in his 1974 model: i.e. an absence of credit constraints (and linked to that a set of identical economic agents).

To which one can advance the simple reply that such theorists have presumably never been unemployed, nor experienced negative equity, nor tried to run a business during a recession, nor indeed tried to set up a new business or entirely fund their own training and education. Credit rationing is among the most important features of any real world economy. And in this respect, the applied business economist may well have a better grip on the issues than does the academic economist.

This line of reasoning implies that, so long as households and companies are credit constrained, a role probably does exist for activist fiscal policies.[9] One strand of thinking that goes on from there is that the more that can be done to liberalise capital markets the better, since doing so reduces an economy's reliance on fiscal adjustments. This is a sensible view that can be taken to stupid extremes; and some would claim that the International Monetary Fund, for one, has done just that.[10] It also implies that in economies that are already performing reasonably close to their full resource utilisation, periods of financial liberalisation should be accompanied by fiscal deflations. Two Chancellors, Tony Barber and Nigel Lawson, would have been more successful had they realised this at the time. Instead, Lawson in particular responded to excessively rapid credit expansion by raising interest rates – a policy that merely drove private sector debt higher still, precipitating a crisis that a fiscal response might have avoided.

The question remains as to just how much fiscal activism is appropriate. The point has been made that borrowing in a growing economy makes more sense than borrowing in an economy that is permanently (not just temporarily) becalmed (like modern Japan's perhaps, where fiscal reflation appears to achieve little). And the subsidiary point has also been made that borrowing to fund growth via investment makes more sense still. The first argument can be put in more precise algebraic terms, to show the maximum sustainable rate of growth of public sector debt, given the size of the existing stock of debt, the rate of growth of the economy and the real cost of debt servicing. If this rate of growth of debt is exceeded, then the stock of debt and the cost of servicing the debt do not simply rise: they spiral up at an accelerating pace. The second point can also be made more precise, if the notion of 'investment' itself can be made less arbitrary, and if the returns on public sector investment can be assessed with suitable rigour.

All of which brings us right into the middle of Gordon Brown's fiscal policy, with its emphasis on medium- to long-term sustainability and on borrowing to fund investment, not consumption. In the short term the current Chancellor is happy to allow the automatic stabilisers to generate rising budget deficits in recessions and rising surpluses in boom times; but in the medium to long term he is much less indulgent. Furthermore, even in the short term the Chancellor cannot be completely relaxed about extremely large cyclical deficits, since even though temporary, their long-term impact may be quite large. So although the Chancellor's fiscal rules have won him many admirers, it has to be said that he has been lucky in his timing, and has not yet had to face serious economic adversity.

Gordon Brown also has his critics, including some who dislike the redistributive nature of many of his tax changes, and others who criticise him for having initially stuck to his predecessors' spending plans, thereby perhaps impeding essential improvements to key public services such as health, education and transport. Other commentators and politicians offer the opposite criticism: that having been initially cautious on spending, the Chancellor, and presumably the prime minister too, have opted for spending rises at the expense of the fiscal policy formulae. At heart Gordon Brown is a politician not a parson: if he has to sacrifice either the spending or the fiscal rules he will, his critics say, shed the rules.

It may seem inappropriate to make such points, which are not merely political but indeed journalistic in their nature, in what purports to be a discussion of economic issues. There is, however, a justification and an important one. In the last decade economic theorists have realised (maybe that should be 'rediscovered') that the issue of policy credibility can be crucial to the issue of policy effectiveness. This is most commonly referred to in the context of monetary policy, and it provides the rationale for central bank independence; but the same is true in the fiscal arena, with some significant implications.

A basic point is that fiscal tightening is generally taken more seriously by the financial markets than is monetary tightening. As a result, when governments run into trouble with their economic policies and experience a collapse in confidence, their response is usually to use a tightening of fiscal policy as the central element in rebuilding confidence. That was true in 1966 and after the 1967 devaluation, and again in 1976, and it was true in the period following the 1992 exchange-rate mechanism (ERM) crisis. In the latter case it occurred after a monetary tightening – in the form of four percentage points on base rates – had made the crisis worse, not better.

In 1976 the crisis of confidence had two linked elements. One was a perception that public spending was spiralling out of control, and pushing the Labour administration into a situation in which public sector debt would accumulate at an explosive rate. This perception was partly generated by Treasury forecasts for the public sector borrowing requirement which have since been shown to have been too pessimistic: a fact which the Chancellor of the time, Denis Healey, subsequently latched on to and used to imply that the 1976 IMF crisis was partly the fault of the Treasury's poor forecasters.[11] But the second element of the crisis was a perception that these fiscal problems were a symptom of a deeper malaise, in which the Labour administration was losing control over the conduct of government, including but not confined to unrealistic pay settlements in the public sector and an unnecessary level of recruitment of public sector staff. The Chancellor, like every other minister, was perceived to be part of the problem; the IMF, precisely because it was an outsider, was part of the solution.

The Gordon Brown Treasury regime has been determined not to repeat that mistake. The present Chancellor's fearsome reputation within government, and his unpopularity among other ministers, is in that context an advantage: he has a credibility in the financial markets that Denis Healey completely lacked in 1976 and then struggled to acquire. But more important to this credibility are the fiscal policy arrangements that Brown has put in place. His fiscal formula has more plausibility than earlier versions, partly because it allows for temporary fluctuations around medium- to long-term sustainability, but also because the Treasury has agreed to an unprecedented degree of transparency, and to independent scrutiny of its arithmetic. It really is very hard for the Chancellor to cheat.

That does not, unfortunately, mean that it is impossible for Gordon Brown or his successors to get it wrong. In this regard the last half-decade has been rather unusual by post-war standards, since the recent tendency has been for public spending to undershoot rather than to over-shoot (whereas tax revenues are on average equally likely to be above or below expectations). And as a generalisation it is probably right to say that the control of spending is now as good as it has ever been. But the path to where we are now has been rather a long one, and the path from here on may not be as easy as the Treasury likes to imply.

A rational set of principles with which to exercise spending control might be the following: that the amount of available resources should determine the scale of the spending plans, and not vice versa; that decisions on this require a clear exercise of collective responsibility from Cabinet; and that effective mechanisms should be found with which to implement the plans, once they are agreed. Another obvious principle might be that all spending decisions should take place in nominal not in real terms – i.e. that spending should not be allowed to rise in nominal terms just because inflation is coming through above expectations. Yet the first three of these were not accepted until 1961, when the report of the Plowden Committee laid them out, and the fourth was not accepted for another decade and a half, until Denis Healey introduced cash limits.

Hugh Dalton's frustrations in this regard have already been referred to, and in 1958 Peter Thorneycroft resigned the Chancellorship, when he lost patience with the refusal of his Cabinet colleagues to curtail their spending ambitions. Before that Hugh Gaitskell had nearly resigned the job on Budget Day 1950, when

Nye Bevan attempted to get Cabinet to veto Gaitskell's proposed introduction of health charges; Gaitskell won the last-minute support of his prime minister, Clement Attlee, which Peter Thorneycroft failed to receive from his leader, Harold Macmillan.

Such traumas are much less likely to happen now. There has been a gradual shift towards tighter and more professional management of public spending, especially under the 1979–97 Conservative governments and their Labour successor.[12] If there is a problem it is more likely to be a chronic than an acute one: that transport, health and education will all cost far more to fix than the Treasury dares admit, or that the provision of state pensions will need to be raised way above what is currently planned, or simply that sustained economic recession will damage the fiscal balance over a correspondingly sustained period.

The issues here are as usual partly political and partly economic. Take pensions. Since the late 1980s, governments of both major political parties have sought to encourage individuals to fund their own pensions, and to rely neither on their employers nor on the state to make full provision on their behalf. Yet the evidence suggests that most people are not saving enough to give them anything like the post-retirement living standards that they themselves expect. So future political pressures for very large increases in the state pension could be substantial, making the conduct of fiscal policy much harder than it currently seems, and leaving Gordon Brown as the least, not the most, far-sighted of Chancellors.

In this context the point made earlier about fiscal policy being a device for redistributing people's incomes through time may need to be modified, since there may be a bit of game-playing going on too. If future state pensions turn out to be generous but means tested, then the rational thing for the individual to do now is to under-provide for retirement – and that is what a good independent financial adviser ought to suggest. If future state pensions will not be generous, then the best policy for the individual is to save heavily. For the Treasury, it is rational to insist that the second outcome will prevail, even if privately it accepts that the first is more likely. So perhaps transparency is not so well established, after all.

A similar perspective, but operating across nations rather than across time, can be applied to the biggest fiscal policy issue of our time: the fiscal implications that would ensue if the United Kingdom were to participate fully in European Monetary Union. One of the more rational arguments against participation is that the fiscal rules to which participants must adhere are unreasonably stringent – so much so that there is a real puzzle as to why the system's designers opted for them at all. Certainly the requirement in the Stability and Growth Pact of a balanced or surplus budget over the course of the economic cycle, and a maximum deficit at any one time of 3 per cent of GDP, is stricter than Gordon Brown's Golden Rule. And the fact that participating countries have to obey the fiscal rule while forgoing the possibility of a partially offsetting monetary boost or currency depreciation (since interest rates are set by the European Central Bank or ECB) makes acceptance of the Pact seem stranger still.

Advocates of the system regard this criticism as a wilful missing of the point. It is precisely because the Pact encourages all participants towards fiscal stringency that the ECB can confidently opt for a relaxed monetary policy. And indeed, there is a rather pretty debating point to be scored here. British opponents of euro membership say that it would be just like ERM membership only worse, and that withdrawal from the ERM in 1992 produced an upturn in the British economy that has already lasted for a decade and which shows no signs of faltering. But the post-1992 policy has essentially been one of fiscal parsimony and monetary relaxation, which is precisely what the euro system allegedly provides. Thus the 'antis' are snookered by their own evidence.

There is also an argument, which has some strength, that fiscal 'freedom' is entirely illusory in any country that has a long history of large budget deficits, and which is now having to accommodate itself to globalised capital markets. This is not, to be fair, particularly relevant to the UK today, but it would have been directly applicable back in the late 1970s when Denis Healey was being given his instructions by the IMF, while refusing to countenance UK membership of the ERM.

But the real reason for the toughness of the stability pact may be this. What EMU requires is that countries make genuine attempts to tighten fiscal policy when it is needed. But with a common European currency, and hence large fiscal policy spillovers between nations, each individual country has more incentive than before to hope that its neighbours will opt for severe fiscal tightening, while it cheats and takes less action than it should. So there is an inbuilt bias in EMU towards an insufficiently tight fiscal policy.[13] Of course, if the system for imposing discipline, through fines and the like, is convincing, then there is no problem – but it is not. So going for an over-tight fiscal rule, but expecting some falling short, is a realistic way of trying to bring about the scale of fiscal responsibility that is really needed.

There is an obvious problem with this account, which is that if the ECB does not realise that the fiscal rule is partly a bluff, then it will respond to fiscal underperformance by opting for a tighter monetary policy than it would otherwise choose. And even if the ECB is wise to what is going on, the financial markets may not be, and may cause equivalent problems of their own. More generally, any strategy of saying one thing while meaning another carries a large risk. The Stability and Growth Pact could be just that, but it could equally be the instability and stagnation pact – and then not a pact at all.

Notes

1   Director of futures research at economic consultancy Experian Business Strategies and author of *Second Amongst Equals – Chancellors of the Exchequer and the British Economy*, and *The Reluctant Superpower – a History of America's Global Economic Reach*.

2   Fuller discussions of many of the points made in this chapter are contained in *Second Amongst Equals: Chancellors of the Exchequer and the British Economy*, Profile Books, London, 2001, and especially in the more detailed works referred to in that book.

3   Dalton was not concerned about the size of the fiscal deficit, since there was not one, but about the real claim on resources of rising government spending when supply was constrained. But the supply constraint merely reflected an overseas financing constraint, to which the domestic counterpart was a corporate sector financial deficit.

4   Many scholars have observed that the pre-1947 Treasury was always more sympathetic to the Keynesian view, and Keynes more sympathetic to the Treasury view, than summary accounts allow; and that the 1947 Keynesian victory was far from total. It would be surprising if it were otherwise. See, for example, Peter Clarke, *The Keynesian Revolution in the Making 1924–1936*, Clarendon Press, Oxford, 1988, and Robert Skidelsky, *John Maynard Keynes: Fighting for Britain 1937–1946*, Macmillan, London, 2000.

5   The expression was Edwin Plowden's and was used by Chris Bryant as the title of his biography.

6   R. J. Barro, 'Are government bonds net wealth?', *Journal of Political Economy*, vol. 82, no. 6, 1974, pp. 1,095–1,117.

7   Although since there is still a balanced budget multiplier, the effect is non-zero.

8   This assumes that the only alternative to taxation is bond finance: even advocates of this model accept that monetary financing will be reflationary, while some would argue that in liquidity terms bond financing is a lot closer to money financing than to tax financing.

9   The argument here is a simplified version of that in C. J. Allsopp, 'The Assessment: strategic policy dilemmas for the 1980s', *Oxford Review of Economic Policy*, vol. 9, no. 3, autumn 1993, pp. 1–25.

10 The World Bank's former chief economist, Joseph Stiglitz, has provided a broader and richer critique of the IMF than this; and his critique has been just as richly attacked – q.v. Joseph Stiglitz, *Globalisation and its Discontents*, Allen Lane, London, 2002.

11 Denis Healey, *The Time of My Life*, Michael Joseph, London, 1989.

12 The early years of the Thatcher government were marked by historically rapid increases in public spending, partly because the administration had agreed to honour large increases in public sector pay and partly because recession boosted welfare payments (and also cut tax revenues). This encouraged the Treasury to work harder to control spending. The same happened during the Lamont Chancellorship, and reforms were introduced on which the Labour government was able to build.

13 This argument is a modified presentation of that in C. J. Allsopp and D. Vines, 'The Assessment: Macroeconomic Policy after EMU', *Oxford Review of Economic Policy*, vol. 14, no. 3, autumn 1998, pp. 1–23, where the emphasis is on the operation of automatic fiscal stabilisers.

8

FROM NATIONALISATION THROUGH DEREGULATION TO REREGULATION: THE CHANGING BUSINESS CLIMATE

Colin Robinson [1]

I began work as a business economist in 1957, joining the Business Economists Group (forerunner of the Society of Business Economists) in 1958. For about eleven years, before moving into the academic world, I was involved in applying economic analysis to business problems. Most of the work I did was typical of what was done by most business economists of the time [2] – I made economic forecasts and related company activities to them and I gave policy advice to the board. Then, in my last three years, I helped negotiate a long-term contract for the sale of natural gas from one of the first North Sea fields.

The interventionist years

As much of my time was spent in the oil industry, I can most easily illustrate the business climate of the time by reference to that industry, which was in a sector of the economy (energy) where government intervention was particularly intrusive. The other energy industries – electricity generation and supply (including hydro and later nuclear power), gas distribution through pipes and coal mining – had been nationalised in the 1940s: government was therefore involved in setting financial targets for them and gradually became drawn more and more into their activities, instead of confining itself to policy issues as had been the original intention of the founding fathers of nationalisation such as Herbert Morrison.[3] From the late 1950s onwards, governments began the programme of support for British coal mining that continued for another 30 years and which, along with efforts to promote civil nuclear power, dominated policy in the energy sector.[4] The programme was carried out primarily by leaning on the Central Electricity Generating Board to burn more coal and to build more nuclear power stations than it would freely have chosen.

Obviously there were significant indirect effects on the oil industry from the protection of its competitors. But governments intervened more directly, in the spirit of those times. For instance, they persuaded oil companies to site refineries in remote locations as part of their regional policies, and to minimise imports of finished oil products, importing more crude oil for refining in Britain than they would otherwise have done. In 1961 they placed a tax on fuel and heating oils, equivalent to about 40 per cent of the then price of fuel oil, which helped shelter coal. To an extent, the oil companies were indirectly helped by coal protection – for example, successive governments banned imports of coal and Russian oil, thus keeping up the energy price level. In this highly interventionist regime, there was something for all energy producers, though some were more favoured than others.[5] Later, when the North Sea was being developed in the 1960s, politicians and civil servants devised a regime that made the nationalised gas industry de facto monopsonist for British offshore gas.[6]

Outside the energy sector, from the end of World War II to the late 1970s British governments also intervened extensively. At the macroeconomic level, fiscal fine-tuning was in vogue: most macroeconomists evidently believed it was relatively straightforward to 'run' the economy by manipulating government expenditure and taxation. The effects on business of the resultant 'stop-go' cycles were substantial.

At the level of individual industries and firms, a few examples will demonstrate how involved governments were. Large companies were supposed to plan their investment on the assumption of 4 per cent per annum growth in real GDP under the National Plan of the 1960s, an ill-fated exercise in 'indicative planning'; incomes policies were periodically introduced; industrial policies subsidised technologies favoured by ministers and civil servants; failing companies were baled out; governments directed investment into particular sectors of the economy and into particular regions. It made little difference whether a Labour or a Conservative government was in office. The business climate was such that corporations, both private and nationalised, before making major decisions such as how much to invest and where, habitually tried to second-guess what government might think. The potential returns from extracting favours from the relevant politician or civil servant often seemed greater than the returns from product, marketing or other innovation and, not surprisingly, resources flowed into lobbying.

A changed business climate?

The contrast with today's business climate appears remarkable. To take just the most obvious symptoms of change, the government now eschews fiscal fine-tuning, leaving an independent Bank of England as the prime controller of the macroeconomy, subject to a government-set inflation target; the exchange rate is permitted to float; exchange control has gone; regional policies, industrial policies, incomes policies and indicative planning have virtually disappeared, so there is much less direct government involvement in business decisions; the industries nationalised in the 1940s have been denationalised and there has been some further small extension of privatisation; private enterprise has been permitted at the edges of the state education system, the National Health Service and local authority services; labour laws have been fundamentally reformed, one result of which has been a dramatic decline in strike activity.

Underlying all these changes is the frequently heard claim that 'everyone believes in markets now'. Planning is regarded as passé and both major political parties say they prefer to let markets work. The transition from a period, some three decades ago, when government intruded into so many areas of business to the present, apparently much different business climate is worth examination. The rest of this chapter considers briefly some of the root causes of the transition, and then discusses the extent to which the change is real and whether the days of widespread government intervention might return.

A new semi-consensus?

Such an apparently drastic change in the climate in which British business operates suggests that, beneath the surface, there has been a near-revolution in ideas about the respective roles of governments and markets. Certainly the prevailing view in the economics profession has shifted, in line with the 'counter-revolution' against the ideas of the followers of Keynes and against interventionist ideas more generally. Of course, the range of opinions among economists about issues such as 'planning versus markets' is and always has been huge. But it seems clear enough that the views of the median economist have moved towards a new 'semi-consensus', as David Henderson has aptly described it,[7] characterised by the belief that markets should be allowed scope to operate, primarily because of their efficiency advantages, usually tempered by a continuing tendency to search for market 'failures' and to recommend government action to counter them.[8]

Behind these changes in the prevailing view among economists were the following important developments in the subject:

- a much more sceptical attitude towards the efficacy of government macroeconomic policy than in the earlier post-war years, born partly of experience of failure but also because of the growth of a powerful and influential school of monetary economics led by Milton Friedman. Most 'monetarists' would prefer to reduce the scope for discretionary action to 'run' the economy.

- growing doubts about the benefits of government action because of the work of the public choice school, principally in the United States. The writings of James Buchanan, Gordon Tullock and others argued that politicians and civil servants are likely to have similar motivations of self-interest to their private sector counterparts.[9] The assumption that they are wise and disinterested servants of the public good is thus unlikely to yield useful predictions of the outcome of government action. Widespread government failure should be expected.

- a revival of 'Austrian' economic ideas by economists such as Friedrich Hayek and later, in the United States, Israel Kirzner and his followers. Austrian economics is a particularly fundamental critique of microeconomic intervention because it refuses to accept that the perfect competition paradigm, at the heart of much economic thinking, is helpful for policy purposes. Austrians see competition as a dynamic process which takes place over time: most supposed 'failures' are integral parts of the market process with which we tamper at our peril.

These new developments in economics were often transmitted to a wider public than specialist economists by 'think tanks' such as the Institute of Economic Affairs (IEA), which persuaded authors to write papers, accessible to a wide audience, explaining their main ideas and the policy implications. Similar organisations, many of them based on the IEA, have appeared in the United States and elsewhere and appear to have had considerable influence on policy-makers.[10]

The influence of events

A change in prevailing ideas is a necessary but not sufficient con-
dition for economic policy to change. Governments may or may
not be attracted by the new ideas per se. They will be moved to
alter policies if they perceive electoral advantage in doing so.
Given the short time horizons of governments in representative
political systems with elections every few years, prospective electoral gains have to be short-term if they are to be politically
appealing: governments do not want to take actions whose benefits will accrue to their successors. Usually, crisis-like events have
to convince government that there is a practical need for changes
that will yield at least some of their political benefits before the
end of its term.

The collapse of communism was clearly one such event. As
former communist regimes embraced elements of capitalism, and
at the same time revealed the economic decay that had been
hidden for so many years by secretive systems employing dis-
torted statistics, Western political parties that had previously been
half-hearted about capitalism realised there might be political and
economic advantage in allowing markets greater freedom to
operate.

In Britain, change came earlier, preceding the collapse of communism by almost a decade as failures were perceived in the
interventionist measures employed by governments of both major
parties up to the late 1970s. By then, the British economy was
close to crisis, with rampant inflation, recession, serious disruption of public services in the 'winter of discontent' and underlying
disillusionment with the results of nationalisation and the general
direction of economic and industrial policies in the previous 30
years. One result was the election of the second reforming government of the post-war period (the first having been Clement
Attlee's in 1945). The Thatcher administrations from 1979
onwards, impressed by the thinking of liberal market economists,
set out on a programme of economic reform that transformed
policy towards business. Labour, out of office for many years,

eventually came to accept most of the Thatcher reforms: since 1997 Labour has seemed intent on stressing the benefits of competitive markets and the strict limits on successful government intervention.

The conversion of New Labour is especially significant since it demonstrates the extent to which liberal market ideas had been accepted in Britain by the late 1990s. A political party underwent a radical conversion to a new set of ideas presumably because it perceived that a new political agenda had been established to which it must conform if it wished to survive.

A permanent shift in ideas?

But how deeply are liberal ideas now entrenched? Can the end to the war of ideas between supporters of markets and proponents of government intervention now be declared? Has the market view triumphed, or have the last 30 years seen just another temporary victory in a battle, following which combat will be resumed? History suggests the latter. Rather than there having been a permanent shift in favour of the advocates of market forces, it is much more likely that the change has been cyclical and that the ideas that used to give rise to direct government intervention in the economy will resurface in different form. Indeed, they are already reappearing.

Government expenditure

The first item that should give one pause in declaring victory for the market-forces school is the trend of government spending and taxation. For all the changes in business climate outlined above, there has been surprisingly little change in the relative size of government, measured as government expenditure or taxation as a share of gross domestic product (GDP).[11] In the late 1960s, at the apparent height of interventionism, general government expenditure was about 40 per cent of gross domestic product: having risen and then fallen in the intervening years, it is 40 per cent today and expected to rise over the next few years as spending on health and education increases sharply. Tax revenues and compulsory social contributions were just over 35 per cent of GDP in the late 1960s: today they are slightly higher and expected to edge upwards in the near future.[12]

Despite the privatisation and deregulation of recent years, the relative size of government has not altered much because other areas of government spending have grown fast. The old industrial and regional support programmes have virtually gone, defence spending has been cut sharply as a proportion of total government spending, but the expansion of other government activities has more than offset these reductions. Expansion of the welfare state, in particular, has been hard to contain. Rising incomes have stimulated a demand for services zero-priced at the point of delivery, producing excess demand and its symptoms – for example, queueing (as in the National Health Service) and complaints about quality. Governments, in response, have therefore periodically ratcheted up spending, as Labour did in 2001–2, in the almost certainly vain hope of catching up with demand for services to which no prices are attached. Two-thirds of government spending is now for 'social protection', education and health,[13] much of it not on public goods in the accepted sense of goods that are non-excludable and non-rivalrous. More traditional functions of government, such as maintaining law and order and providing defence, are now minor elements of the total.

Government cannot be said to have withdrawn significantly from the economy when its spending and its tax revenues are still equivalent to around 40 per cent of GDP and rising. Government is less involved in direct intervention in the wider economy but its relative size, as measured by spending and taxation, appears undiminished. There are now some efforts to stop that relative size increasing. For example, as explained earlier, private funds are being sought to try to contain soaring government spending on education and health and some still publicly owned transport services (such as London Underground). Unless substantial private funds are obtained, the tax burden will increase and so will the relative size of government.

Government regulation

One popular myth is that British governments in recent years, and especially the Conservatives under Mrs (now Lady) Thatcher, have been deregulators. It is true that some deregulation has occurred, mainly in some of the privatised utilities where the uncertainties of regulation by nationalisation have been replaced by a mix of competitive markets and regulation. But, in general, the story of recent times has been one of growing regulation by government, much of it 'social' (for instance, on environmental, health and safety and worker and investor protection grounds). Much regulation involves only minor amounts of expenditure by government and so is not a significant factor in the growth of government spending.

The growth of government regulation is a very important worldwide phenomenon. National governments constantly promise to reduce the burden of regulation, international organisations such as the OECD complain about the growth of regulation,[14] yet it seems hard to stop. In Britain, despite the efforts of various worthy bodies, such as the Better Regulation Task Force, the annual total of statutory instruments seems to show an inexorably rising trend: it has almost trebled since 1979, with most of the increase since the late 1980s.

The conventional view of regulation appears to be that it is driven by 'public interest' considerations. Yet it is hard to see what would justify such an assumption if one takes the view, with public choice theorists, that those in governments (and government regulatory bodies) have their own interests and tend to seek personal, organisational and political advantage. Regulation is a big subject[15] but the problem can be simplified by examining it from two points of view – first, its intellectual basis, and second the factors that, in practice, drive governments to regulate.

The intellectual basis for regulation

An apparent intellectual basis for government regulation (a 'licence to regulate') is provided by mainstream neo-classical economists. If one takes the mainstream view that perfect competition – or, more precisely, the long-run equilibrium of perfect competition – represents an ideal at which policy should aim, since that ideal is unattainable the way is open for government regulation of virtually all markets. Governments can intervene directly, for example to impose marginal cost pricing, or to break up companies with apparent market power, or less directly to internalise apparent externalities, in the name of correcting market imperfections and failures.

But are these imperfections and failures real, given that they represent departures from an idealised conceptual state that can never be achieved in practice? Perfect markets imply perfect knowledge; since the relevant knowledge for decision-making is always about the future, perfect knowledge can never be obtained. Exercises to determine whether or not markets are 'imperfect' and 'fail' are therefore what Harold Demsetz has aptly described as 'Nirvana economics'.[16] Instead of comparing states of the world that might exist, such exercises instead compare the status quo with an idealised and unrealisable situation and must inevitably conclude that the former falls short of the ideal. It is unhelpful and misleading, from a policy point of view, to describe as 'failures' elements that are an integral part of all known markets.

This is where the 'Austrian' view mentioned earlier provides especially useful insights. Austrian economists (following the old classical tradition) see the long-run equilibrium of perfect competition as unhelpful as a policy guide, arguing that it represents not competition but a state in which competition has been exhausted. To understand markets they would argue that competition should be seen as a dynamic discovery process in which entrepreneurs constantly seek new opportunities, driven by the profit motive.[17] Provided entry to markets is relatively free, the competitive process can be allowed to operate virtually unhindered by government action except that which maintains a framework of law and order, establishes and protects property rights and defends the realm. Only when markets are hampered by government obstacles to entry (so that monopolies appear which cannot be undermined by entry) are problems likely to arise.

The driving forces of regulation

Even if one does not go as far as the Austrians, by examining the drivers of regulation, on the demand side and on the supply side, it can be shown that there are powerful tendencies towards over-regulation in Britain and other 'advanced' economies.

On the demand side, regulation usually appears to consumers to be free at the point of delivery. Consumers do not directly see the costs of a regulation which, for example, 'protects' consumers of financial products by imposing more rules on the product suppliers, nor the costs of rules that impose environmental obligations on companies, nor the costs of working time, holiday or parental leave regulations stemming from the European Union. Demand is therefore likely to exceed what it would be if the costs were more apparent.

The demand for regulation also arises from the activities of pressure groups which, as public choice theorists have pointed out, are major influences on government policies. Since the work of George Stigler more than 30 years ago,[18] it has been recognised that producer groups may demand regulation – for instance, incumbents may seek regulation to keep out smaller rivals on whom the costs would be more onerous – and that producers, with access to most of the information regulators need, may capture regulators. Today the range of pressure groups that seek regulation is much wider:[19] not just producers, but environmental bodies, health and safety interests, trade unions, special-interest consumer groups and others may influence and possibly capture governments and government regulatory bodies. The well-known phenomenon of concentrated benefits and dispersed costs induces interest groups to strive for regulations that will benefit their members. If they can impose their own views on the rest of the community via the medium of government, they will reap considerable rewards: the benefits will be concentrated on their members whereas the costs will be dispersed throughout the community. Thus there is constant pressure on government to pass regulations favourable to one group or another and, since these groups have much of the information necessary to judge the value of regulating, their lobbying seems to be one of the main drivers of regulation.

On the supply side, politicians are particularly prone to regulate. In the face of some difficulty that has arisen (concerning, for instance, an accident or a health scare) a new regulation gives the appearance of being busy in trying to solve the problem. Moreover, regulation has the great political advantage over other action that the costs fall primarily on others.[20] Companies and consumers will bear these costs, in proportions depending on the price elasticity of demand. When an activity is undertaken by people who know they will not bear the bulk of the costs (which are therefore externalities), the classic situation arises in which the activity is likely to be over-expanded.

As far as Britain is concerned, a complication is that, as well as domestic regulators, it has an external supplier of regulation in the form of the European Union (EU). Because of the significant differences among member states, the desire of the EU central authorities to harmonise results in a constant flow of regulation which is then adapted (and in some cases embellished) by the British civil service.

There are other reasons why government regulation tends to expand. For example, regulatory bodies, like other organisations, have empire-building tendencies but, unlike companies in competitive markets, there are no clear constraints on their expansion. Second, regulations almost invariably have unintended consequences: governments then add other regulations intended to correct the effects of the first set.

Conclusions

There is now a vastly improved climate in Britain for doing business compared with my time as a business economist when government dominated economic activity. But, without belittling the efforts of those involved in the transformation, it is as well to look deeper. Government has not been shrinking: on balance, its relative size has changed little in the last 30 years, even though the composition of its activities has altered with a bias towards health, education and welfare. Moreover, government activities that impinge on business are now more subtly deployed. Instead of crude old-style interventionism, regulation by government departments or specially created regulatory bodies is the norm. It is commonly argued that markets should be allowed to operate but, because they fail, only within limits set by the regulators. In some cases, where regulators have adopted a strong pro-competition stance, as in the privatised gas and electricity industries, they have succeeded in opening up markets to competition. But, more generally, regulators have expanded their empires, imposing compliance costs on regulated companies and also constraining entrepreneurship: that constraint, though its effect is hard to measure, is probably the principal cost of regulation.

Rules are necessary if business life (as personal life) is to flourish, but they do not need to be set by government. For centuries rules of business life have evolved, being tested and filtered over time to produce robust norms of behaviour. Furthermore, companies have strong incentives to regulate their own activities to preserve and enhance their reputations. Competitive advantage results from producing what consumers want – in terms, *inter alia*, of products that are safe, healthy and environmentally benign – and in providing good working conditions.[21] Nevertheless, in recent years governments have intervened more and more in rule-setting despite the flawed intellectual basis for this kind of intervention. There are powerful forces at work which generate more regulation over time and which tend to produce over-regulation rather than satisfying some genuine public interest.

There is a danger in the size and growth of regulation which goes beyond the immediate impact on those concerned. In the end, increasing regulation may well lead to a regulatory state where government intrudes by rule-setting into most areas of activity, personal and organisational. The regulatory state might not be much different from the centrally planned state, which practically everyone now, quite rightly, regards as having been a failure wherever it has been tried. It has been inefficient and it has imposed unacceptable restrictions on personal freedom. Yet the regulatory state would face very similar problems. As in central planning, a small number of people would be the decision-makers. Like would-be central planners, regulators would face a serious deficiency of information because, as Hayek pointed out, central authorities cannot collect the dispersed information that is produced by markets.[22] Decision-making would be largely arbitrary.

In summary, triumphalism about the acceptance of market forces is misplaced. There is a creep back towards the interventionism of the past, albeit in new forms. Government spending on goods and services other than public goods tends to run away as consumers react in the ways economists would predict. And the forces that are producing rising regulation are powerful indeed. Only if some of the goods and services now provided by government are returned to private sector suppliers, and if government fundamentally changes its attitude to regulation by recognising that it should not aim to be the prime rule-setter for the community, are market ideas likely to grow deep roots.

Notes

1   Professor of Economics, University of Surrey.
2   The work of business economists in the late 1960s is surveyed in a volume produced in association with the Business Economists Group – K. J. W. Alexander, A. G. Kemp and T. M. Rybczynski (eds), *The Economist in Business*, Blackwell, 1967.

3   See A. H. Hanson (ed.), *Nationalisation: A Book of Readings*, Allen and Unwin, 1963, especially Chapter II.

4   Colin Robinson, *A Policy for Fuel?*, Occasional Paper 31, Institute of Economic Affairs, 1969, and *Energy Policy: Errors, Illusions and Market Realities*, Occasional Paper 93, Institute of Economic Affairs, 1993.

5   Robinson, *A Policy for Fuel?*, op. cit.

6   Colin Robinson and Jon Morgan, *North Sea Oil in the Future: Economic Analysis and Government Policy*, Macmillan, 1978, and Colin Robinson, 'The Errors of North Sea Policy', *Lloyds Bank Review*, no. 141, July 1981.

7   David Henderson, *The Changing Fortunes of Economic Liberalism*, Occasional Paper 105, Institute of Economic Affairs, 1998.

8   Colin Robinson, 'Energy Economists and Economic Liberalism', *The Energy Journal*, vol. 21, no. 2, 2000.

9   For an explanation see, for example, Gordon Tullock, Arthur Seldon and Gordon Brady, *Government: Whose Obedient Servant?*, Readings 51, Institute of Economic Affairs, 2000.

10 Richard Cockett, *Thinking the Unthinkable: Think Tanks and the Economic Counter Revolution*, HarperCollins, 1994.

11 On difficulties in measuring the relative size of government in the economy, see David B. Smith, 'How High Is Tax? How Big Is Spend?', in Peter Warburton (ed.), *IEA Yearbook of Government Performance, 2002/2003*, Institute of Economic Affairs, 2002, Chapter 1.

12 See Warburton, op. cit., especially Charts Part 1.

13 Ibid.

14 *Focus*, Public Management Gazette, no. 8, OECD, March 1998, p. 1.

15 John Blundell, Colin Robinson et al., *Regulation without the State: The Debate Continues*, Readings 52, Institute of Economic Affairs, 2000, deals with the issues in more detail.

16 H. Demsetz, 'Information and Efficiency: Another Viewpoint', *Journal of Law and Economics*, vol. 12, no. 1, 1969, and *Efficiency, Competition and Policy*, Blackwell, 1989.

17   F. A. Hayek, 'The Meaning of Competition', in *Individualism and Economic Order*, George Routledge and Sons, 1948, and Israel M. Kirzner, *The Meaning of Market Process*, Routledge, 1992.

18   George J. Stigler, 'The Theory of Economic Regulation', *Bell Journal of Economics and Management*, spring 1971.

19   Sam Peltzman, 'Towards a More General Theory of Regulation', *Journal of Law and Economics*, August 1976.

20   One US study indicates that costs borne by government are only about 2 per cent of the compliance costs of regulation. See Blundell and Robinson, op. cit., p. 5.

21   Daniel B. Klein, *Reputation: Studies in the Voluntary Elicitation of Good Conduct*, University of Michigan Press, 1987.

22   Hayek and Kirzner, op. cit.

9

THE INFLUENCE OF STERLING ON POLICY

Jim O'Neill[1]

In 1953, when the SBE was formed, sterling stood at 2.80 against the dollar, and at just below 12.0 against the Deutschmark. Since then, when its long-term decline began, with accompanying gyrations, sterling has dominated large areas of policy-making, even during times when the pound was not explicitly a policy objective.

In fact, for around 24 of those 50 years sterling has been a direct objective of policy. For the remaining 26, it has been 'floating', and other objectives have been formally more important. However, in this latter period movements in sterling have occasionally done enough damage to suggest that the pound can be a headache even when it is not a policy objective.

So what have business economists learnt about sterling from that experience? What lessons are there for the future? Will the UK join EMU?

It seems as though the – admittedly short – experience of the last decade, when sterling was largely ignored and policy-makers concentrated on a credible domestic target, might be a superior policy strategy while sterling retains an independent existence.

For the question of whether in the future the UK should join the single currency, this recent experience suggests that it would be optimal for the UK to join only *if* the credibility of European institutions and their policy-making is superior to that of the UK, and any policy implemented helps the UK satisfy its objectives *better* than the current system. It remains a difficult call, but the case for getting rid of the challenges posed by the pound is perhaps less obvious than it was a few years ago.

As for what business economists may have learnt, I am not sure whether it is that much. Foreign exchange forecasting remains, as it has always been, difficult. In some ways it is more so now with the growth of capital markets, and in particular the growth of the equity culture. Therefore forecasting currencies requires an adaptable framework. For the pound, given the UK's balance of payments peculiarities stemming from the importance of London and the UK in global capital markets, it is especially challenging. We can easily explain and rationalise the movements of sterling *after* they have occurred but the tools to anticipate them reliably remain a secret. If any SBE members discover them in the next 50 years, I would be grateful for a call!

Sterling since 1953

Chart 1 shows that since 1953 sterling has generally declined against the dollar, Deutschmark and on a trade-weighted basis.

As can be seen, the stronger performance of the pound since 1995 barely registers on a long-term chart. This is a shame because a more careful examination reveals that, on a trade-weighted basis, sterling has, in fact, been more stable since 1997, and if this continues for much longer it will start to rival the stability of the 1950s when sterling operated under a fixed exchange-rate regime. Given that 1997 marks the granting to the Bank of England of an independent role in monetary policy, this certainly gives support to the confidence that this government may have acquired from its current strategy.

Before discussing this strategy, it is interesting to look at the long-term history of the UK balance of payments, which may help us to understand the way sterling has changed in value.

Chart 1   **Sterling TWI**

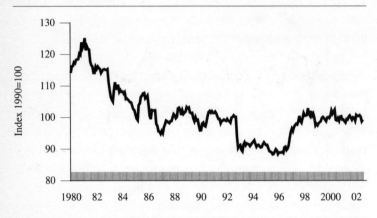

The UK balance of payments since 1953

Chart 2 below is self-explanatory, showing the UK trade and current account balances as a percentage of GDP going back to 1955.

Trade deficits have apparently become a fact of life in the UK. Except for a brief modest surplus at the start of the 1970s and a slightly bigger surplus as a result of North Sea oil in the early 1980s, the trade balance has been firmly in the red. Does this matter? The movement of sterling across the exchanges depends on more than the trade in goods. The UK has played a powerful role in service industries globally, and notably in financial services, and the current account balance reflects this. This has fared better than the trade balance, but has broadly followed the same path and, since the early 1980s, it too has been in persistent deficit. Again the question has to be asked: 'Does it matter?'

On the face of it the period of deficits since 1970 has roughly coincided with the secular decline in the pound. However, before coming to any conclusions it is important to consider the rest of the balance of payments and, in particular, 'quality' flows such as net foreign direct investment and net portfolio flows. This is

Chart 2   **UK: trade balance versus current account**

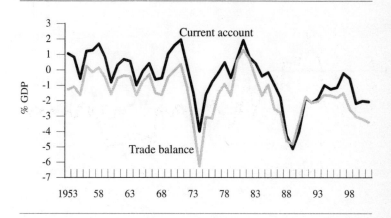

where analysing sterling's behaviour starts to get tricky owing to the size and position of the UK financial services sector. Much of the reported portfolio flows in and out of the UK might not involve purchases and sales of currency. Adding to this complication is the fact that, until foreign exchange controls were entirely lifted in 1979, it is not really clear what importance should be attached to capital flow data. Despite these provisos, Chart 3 below shows the broad basic balance of payments[2] against the sterling trade-weighted index.

Unfortunately, this approach doesn't obviously give a key insight into the behaviour of sterling. While it has been suggested that the long-term weakness of trade-weighted sterling has reflected the general accumulated deficit in the broad balance of payments, the brief periods of reported BBoP surplus are not accompanied by periods of sterling appreciation. Moreover, the significant appreciation of sterling from 1995 to 1997 was followed by a significant decline in the UK BBoP deficit.

Not surprisingly, statistical analysis does not reveal any greater insights. Over the twenty-year period, the correlation coefficient between trade-weighted sterling and the BBoP is 0.14, and a

---

Chart 3   **UK: BBoP versus sterling TWI**

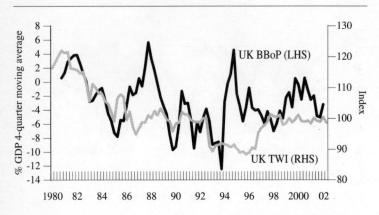

---

simple econometric analysis does not deliver statistically reliable results.

However, a similar analysis of the importance of the BBoP for movements in other major currencies is statistically more robust. For instance, undertaking the same calculation for the US dollar gives a coefficient of 0.21. Also, Chart 4 below shows the euro trade-weighted against the eurozone BBoP, and there appears to be a very good relationship over the euro's short life to date.

The fact that we cannot find statistically significant results for the pound's relationship with the BBoP is quite probably due to the UK's importance as a financial centre, and, as we shall see later, analysis of the factors that drive BBoP developments and the pound might be more rewarding. After all, if the BBoP reflects the underlying commercial or 'sustainable' flows and the remainder of the balance of payments is speculative or hot money flows, it is likely that the trend is determined by the BBoP.

Different policy regimes since 1953

The recently published *Reforming Britain's Economic and*

Chart 4   **Euro area BBoP versus euro TWI**

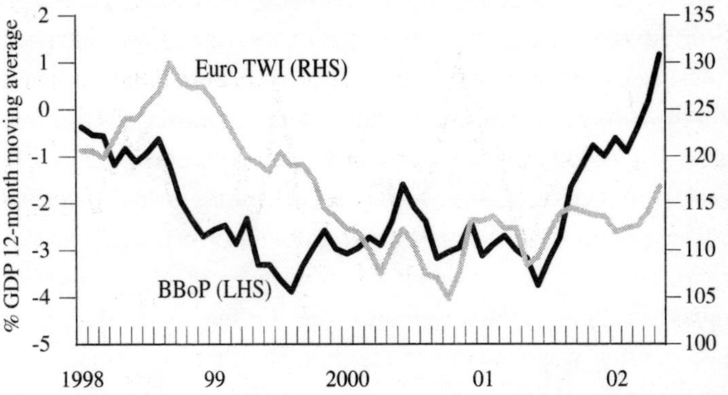

Financial Policy, by Ed Balls and Gus O'Donnell,[3] organises post-war monetary policy regimes into five distinctive periods, and it is useful to examine the part played by the exchange rate in each. I have added the experience of inflation targeting with an independent central bank since 1997 as a sixth point.

Looking at the dates for these periods reveals two when direct exchange-rate targeting was the rule, 1948–71, and 1987–92. The remainder have seen different variations of domestic targets, generally relating to a monetary target before 1987 and an inflation target since 1992. So the 50-year existence of the SBE has seen the exchange rate as a specific target of policy for 24 years, but not targeted for 26 years. Let us now turn briefly to each of the periods identified by Balls and O'Donnell.

1953–71: Bretton Woods
During the period of Bretton Woods,[4] maintenance of a fixed exchange rate against the dollar was the main goal of monetary policy and it is quite remarkable reading the history books to see how specific a constraint on domestic policy the balance of payments current account was at that time. A. J. Prest provides an

extraordinarily detailed analysis of the period in his book *The UK Economy: A Manual of Applied Economics*.[5]

No wonder the alternative attractions of floating exchange rates were seen as a more viable approach for UK government.

The devaluation of the pound's fixed rate from $4.03 to $2.80 in 1949, before the SBE was formed, actually meant that the UK balance of payments had a small trade surplus during the early days of the society. History books tell us that the pound was then kept at an overvalued rate for a significantly extended period. Keynes, in his *The Economic Consequences of Mr Churchill*,[6] famously ridiculed the revaluation of sterling by Churchill in 1925, when it was restored to the gold standard at a higher rate after World War I. This set the UK on a difficult path in the inter-war years, and after the war the reluctance of the authorities to devalue the pound until 1949 shows a very early symptom of a policy error that has been repeated ever since.

Throughout the 1950s, and especially the 1960s, the increasingly poor performance of the UK economy compared to the resurgent Germany and Japan, as well as the resourceful USA, meant that the nation was increasingly coming under a perceived balance of payments constraint, and the forced devaluation in 1967 under Harold Wilson and the Chancellor, James Callaghan, was a surprise only in how long it was in coming.

1971–6: a rudderless era
Bretton Woods began to collapse in 1971 but was only fully abandoned in 1973, resulting in an unpredictable era for international economic policy, with the USA in considerable turmoil. With the oil crisis of 1973–4 contributing to an inflationary era, the global circumstances were hardly favourable to an objective judgement of the success of a new monetary standard. While its Continental neighbours first experimented with a managed float within the so-called 'snake', the UK felt more compelled to the attractions of floating and the idea that UK policy-making would be free of the balance of payments constraint. Six weeks was all the UK could

manage in the 'snake', perhaps a fact that many should have remembered when the UK joined the European Union's Exchange Rate Mechanism (ERM) in 1990!

The period was associated with some of the UK's most turbulent economic days and, with the pound under significant attack by 1976, Prime Minister Callaghan was forced to tighten economic policy even though the balance of payments constraint had been formally removed. The humiliating cancellation of an overseas trip by Chancellor Denis Healey on the insistence of the IMF is a salutary tale for those who think that floating exchange rates necessarily mean no foreign exchange policy!

1976–87: monetary targeting

In many ways, the Callaghan-Healey policy response to the IMF was a key pointer to the next era, which was dominated by the monetarist thinking popularised by Milton Friedman and eagerly implemented by Prime Minister Margaret Thatcher under the guidance of Sir Alan Walters. A floating exchange rate was a *key* cornerstone of this era, although at times the restrictive monetary policy of the late 1970s had seemed almost to look to a rising exchange rate to achieve the goal of significantly lower inflation.

The advent of North Sea oil gave the UK a new asset at a time of significant global oil supply disruptions, and soon afterwards the second oil-price crisis compounded the policy dilemma. In a new departure the strength of the pound was becoming a policy issue. The book *The Money Supply and the Exchange Rate*,[7] edited by Eltis and Sinclair, summarises superbly the many issues that arose from the new-found strength of the pound, which demonstrated quickly that a floating exchange rate did not necessarily allow the luxury of policy disinterest towards sterling. Indeed, this period probably laid the early foundations for the consideration of entry into the ERM. Stephens[8] gives an interesting documentation of how early the question of ERM entry became a widely discussed issue.

At the same time as the Thatcher experiment with monetarism

got under way, President Reagan in the USA was combining an extremely expansionary fiscal policy with a monetarist-based approach to interest rate policy in an attempt to 'shock' inflation expectations out of the system. As a result, the value of the dollar soared in the early 1980s, culminating in the embarrassment of the pound nearly dropping below parity against the dollar. Despite the fact that the dollar had surged against all major currencies, the Thatcher administration was eager to prevent a move below parity, and effectively this brought an end to the era of monetary targets.

The consequences of the rise in the dollar for the US economy subsequently led to the September 1985 Plaza Accord, by which the Group of Five industrialised countries deliberately devalued the dollar. By 1987, the dollar had declined so much that the expanded Group of Seven (G7)[9] attempted to introduce 'target zones' by which the exchange rates of the major currencies were briefly managed within ranges of 2.5 and 5 per cent against the dollar under the Louvre Accord. The willingness of the UK authorities to participate in this arrangement laid the early foundations for Britain's ill-fated life in the ERM.

1987–92: exchange-rate targeting

Throughout the monetarist-driven era of Reagan and Thatcher, the Continental Europeans had persisted with the European Monetary System (EMS) after its introduction in 1978. Eleven member countries of the EU had used the system's Exchange Rate Mechanism to limit the changes in value of the currencies against each other during the dramatic currency turmoil of the early 1980s – the Louvre Accord idea was effectively an attempt to globalise the ERM on a limited basis.

Exchange-rate targeting had therefore been in the background of the Thatcher administration, having been introduced on the Continent just before its arrival in office. Consequently, for UK Chancellors Howe and then Lawson, the idea of making the UK an ERM member and thereby linking monetary policy to that of the Bundesbank, which had established a reputation in financial markets for successful control of inflation, had been an obvious attraction when domestic monetary targets still had no clear anchor. The hostility of the prime minister towards the notion subsequently cost Howe and Lawson their careers, and it was left to John Major to persuade Margaret Thatcher of the virtues of the ERM.

The fact that UK interest rates were reduced on the announcement of UK entry to the ERM on 8 October 1990 gave perhaps an early sign of the perceived benefits of membership. The fact that the UK 'announced' its joining rate of DM2.95 without any consultation with its European partners was a somewhat more blunt indication of how the UK government was thinking. It is of course ironic that at the time of writing markets seem to perceive that the UK could cope with permanent membership of the European Monetary Union, and of the euro, at an exchange rate close to the equivalent of DM2.95. Back in 1990, virtually all independent observers believed that the pound had entered the ERM at an overvalued exchange rate, a decision that would come back to haunt the UK.

Of course, with the collapse of the Berlin Wall in 1989 and the unification of Germany, the external factors were far from ideal for UK participation. In hindsight one still wonders, as many did at the time, whether, if the Deutschmark had been revalued against all currencies in 1990 and both the Italian lira and sterling devalued in early 1992, the turmoil of 1992–4 would have subsequently occurred and the blushes of John Major and Norman Lamont been spared. The inability to deal with the embarrassment of devaluation may ironically have sown the seeds for the post-1992 era and the so-far successful period of inflation targeting.

1992–7: inflation targeting

Hazardous consequences were predicted for the UK after its unceremonious departure from the ERM, but somehow the Major government managed to find new policy levers and, under the stewardship of Ken Clarke, inflation targeting was born. With monetary policy still under the control of the Chancellor, it is not entirely clear whether inflation targeting was initially a public relations exercise to calm fears about post-ERM life, but the plan quickly developed into a coherent framework, in which the open scrutiny of the Chancellor's actions by the Bank of England played an important role. Sterling played little if any part in policy.

1997 onwards: inflation targeting and an independent central bank

The Blair and Brown (New) Labour government took the previous government's framework one giant step farther, shocking financial markets with its announcement on arrival in office in 1997 that the Bank of England would be made independent. With the Monetary Policy Committee charged with keeping inflation, measured by RPIX,[10] within a band of one percentage point on either side of a target rate of 2.5 per cent, the Bank has rarely strayed from its task in the more than five years since. Although the global inflation environment has been benign, the Bank has delivered on its goals, as well as enabling the UK to be among the strongest-growing economies in Europe, as well as in the G7. Moreover, as we showed earlier, sterling has also displayed a remarkable degree of stability on a trade-weighted basis for much of this period. Indeed, given the success of monetary policy in the past five years under an independent Bank of England, it is not surprising that many observers are cynical about the real intentions of this government if it were actually to decide to abandon this framework for the uncertainties of life in EMU.

The future for sterling: is there one?

In between my writing this chapter and its publication, the government will have had to decide whether to hold a referendum on whether the UK should join EMU, thereby potentially getting rid of the pound altogether. Judging by the flavour of the discussion previously and the dominant role that sterling has played in UK policy since 1953, getting rid of sterling might seem a good option. However, it will also mean that we lose our own interest rate policy and our inflation performance will be set by a monetary policy council that does not look after the UK's interests alone, but the collective interests of the eurozone. Sterling would no longer be a constraint on policy but exchange-rate developments would still have a considerable bearing on the UK's economic performance.

Will the UK join? The eventual attractions of a stable currency in relations with our most important trading partners seem worthy of the cause, but other currencies important to the UK, such as the dollar, will still fluctuate in value, and presumably the attractions of membership will be stronger if the eurozone economies, and Germany in particular, are themselves stronger.

Giving up the apparent clarity of the UK monetary framework too early seems risky in view of all sterling's historical problems, and ignoring the exchange rate in favour of a clearly defined inflation target seems like a better option than getting rid of the pound too quickly. Consequently, a referendum in this parliament seems unlikely, although a subsequent third term for the Blair and Brown team might bring a different outcome.

Analysing sterling: what have we learnt?

If there is to be a future for sterling, what have we learnt from the past about its movements and key drivers?

Analysis of the broad basic balance of payments (BBoP) seemed to be useful for the main currencies, and therefore understanding the key influences on the different components of the BBoP will be important. For the UK, with its large international financial services sector, and the pound's position in the cross-fire between the euro and the dollar, it is not at all clear that we have learnt much at all.

Chart 5   **GS TWI: sterling**

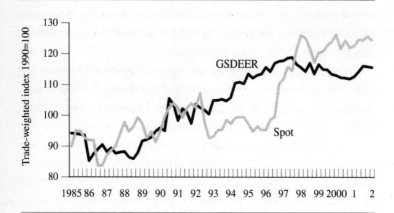

In terms of simple valuation, the pound seems overvalued at current exchange rates according to the procedure we favour most at Goldman Sachs. The Goldman Sachs GSDEER[11] model is constructed using relative productivity and relative inflation rates, and at the time of writing[12] sterling is estimated to be overvalued by around 8 per cent on a trade-weighted basis. Against the euro, it seems more overvalued, by around 17 per cent, but this is largely due to the misalignment of the euro/dollar rate (an issue that would be relevant even within EMU).

It is interesting to observe that after weakening throughout the 1980s and early 1990s the GSDEER for sterling has been stable since the 1997 period, according to our estimates. Whether this is because of the new policy regime since the Bank of England's independence only time will tell, but it has coincided with a period of low and stable inflation and higher, less variable, output than that of most of the UK's important competitors.

Even if this estimate of fair value for sterling is accurate, how useful is it for trading or hedging?

In a long-term model, it is possible to detect the statistical significance of UK current account deficits, but whether this is simply due to the coincidence of sterling's long-term decline and the persistence of current account deficits makes for considerable debate. Worrying about the UK current account deficit would not have helped sterling bears since 1995.

Nevertheless, although we showed earlier that the BBoP has not been statistically significant for sterling in the past, it is hard to suggest any other starting point for SBE members who wish to make a future for themselves forecasting sterling.

The BBoP is derived from the current account, net foreign direct investment and net portfolio flows, both bonds and equities. Consequently, to get sterling 'right' all that is required, in addition to accurate data and an excellent understanding of the euro/dollar rate, is models to predict trends in UK imports, exports and invisible trade, international cross-border mergers and acquisitions, and so on.

Members who can combine the skills of international trade expertise, investment banking and finance theory, modern bond analysis and equity research should be fine. My telephone number is available for those with all the answers!

Notes

1   Head of Global Economics Research, Goldman Sachs. Until September 2001, Jim was co-head and Chief Foreign Currency Economist.

2   The narrow basic balance (NBoP) is defined as the current account plus net foreign direct investment, and the broad basic balance (BBoP) as the NBoP plus net portfolio flows, namely bonds and equities.

3   Ed Balls and Gus O'Donnell (eds), *Reforming Britain's Economic and Financial Policy*, HM Treasury, 2001.

4   See Note 5, Chapter 1 – *Ed*.

5   A. J. Prest, *The UK Economy: A Manual of Applied Economics*, Weidenfeld and Nicolson, 1968.

6   John Maynard Keynes, *The Economic Consequences of Mr Churchill*, Hogarth Press, 1925.

7   W. Eltis and P. Sinclair (eds), *The Money Supply and the Exchange Rate*, Oxford University Press, 1981.

8   P. Stephens, *Politics and the Pound: The Conservatives' Struggle with Sterling*, Macmillan, 1996.

9   The Group of Seven comprised the United States, Japan, Canada, France, Germany, the United Kingdom and Switzerland – *Ed.*

10   Retail Price Index excluding the direct effect of interest rate changes.

11   GSDEER is Goldman Sachs Dynamic Equilibrium Real Exchange Rates. A detailed description can be found in *The Foreign Exchange Book*, September 1996.

12   This article was written in autumn 2002. Since then the pound has declined against the strengthening euro. By May 2003, sterling was only overvalued by around 3 per cent on a trade weighted basis.

10

DOES FORECASTING HAVE A FUTURE?

John Walker[1]

Introduction

Governments, corporations and financial institutions all need forecasts for policy and planning purposes, both internally and to take part in external discussions. There are plenty of forecasts available to use for such purposes. For example, the October 2002 issue of *Consensus Forecasts* lists 22 organisations in its UK section. What is more, most of these forecasts are available at little cost and are frequently updated. Surely these are classic signs of a healthy and successful economic activity? So why is forecasting held in such low esteem and why do we need to ask whether forecasting has a future? My aim in this paper is to try to answer these questions and, in particular, to argue that forecasting using macroeconometric models certainly has a future.

In the next section I illustrate why forecasts are needed, then I describe the different ways forecasts can be made, and the most important changes seen in the forecasting process over the last 30 years. Next I consider why forecasting is so difficult and look at the causes of forecast errors. I go on to discuss how macro-econometric models can be used not only to produce point forecasts but also have an important role in producing variants, scenarios and simulations, and I conclude with some general indications of where I believe forecasting is heading in the future.

Why do we need economic forecasts?

It is easy to see why governments and central banks need forecasts. In the UK the Monetary Policy Committee needs to be able to forecast since its remit is to hit an inflation target and, given the lags with which interest rates affect inflation, it needs to adjust policy to pre-empt any inflationary or deflationary trends. To do this it needs to forecast what inflation would be with no change in interest rates and what any change in rates would do to that inflation forecast. The UK Treasury needs an economic forecast in order to calculate likely tax revenues and public sector borrowing.

But private sector organisations are just as dependent on forecasts. For example, if Marconi had been able to forecast the collapse in telecommunications production, it would have fared much better over the last two years. If financial organisations had been able to foresee that interest rates were to stay at very low levels in 2002, they would have been able to increase their profitability sharply. So forecasting matters a lot to many organisations – and the people involved in these organisations.

Ways of forecasting

Economic forecasts can be made in a number of ways, including the following.

Guessing and related methods using no formal procedures

It is often argued that forecasting without any formal methodology of any kind relies on luck. However, it is possible to argue that even guessing implicitly uses a model, albeit one that is not written down. So, someone with lots of experience may weight a number of factors together to produce a forecast. Such forecasts may do quite well in standard tests.

But there are a number of problems with this approach. First, in a complex world it becomes increasingly difficult, and time-consuming, to cover all the variables needed 'by hand' or on the classic 'back of the envelope'. Second, and more importantly, it is well nigh impossible to calculate reliable variants, or adjust such forecasts rapidly should new information become available. Third, models that exist in your head may be wonderfully flexible, with time-varying parameters and factors that can be added or deleted as appropriate. But that is also their disadvantage. There is a tendency to produce the answer that you already believe to be the case for whatever reason. More formal procedures challenge your hunches and require much more discipline.

Extrapolation of trends

Simple extrapolation can also work well in forecasting so long as recent trends persist – and that is the point. They often do but sometimes, quite critically, they don't, leaving such forecasters badly adrift. Again, we could refer to the unfortunate Marconi experience, in which extrapolation would have egged on the disaster.

Time series models

Time series models often perform well in forecasting tests and are quick and easy to update. However, these sometimes suffer from failures similar to the extrapolative models and typically are not suitable for analysis of policy changes and forecast variants. As soon as these models start to become more complex, they are practically indistinguishable from the mainstream structural econometric models described below.

Survey-based forecasting

Surveys of consumers and businesses are useful, especially for information about the current situation and the very near future. But surveys rarely help for forecasts beyond three to six months ahead.

Standard econometric models

Structural econometric forecasting models are systems of equations that systematically incorporate the relationships between variables such as GDP, inflation, interest rates, unemployment, etc. These relationships are embodied in equations that are estimated from available data, often incorporating restrictions based upon a theoretical knowledge of how economies work. Most of the forecasts produced by governments, academic groups and professional forecasting groups have adopted this approach, and this will be the focus of the rest of the paper.

How forecasting has changed over the last 30 years

I first became involved with economic forecasting almost 30 years ago at the UK Treasury. An impressive group of about 40 economists were using a huge econometric model (of over 1,200 variables) to produce regular forecasts just for the UK economy. Many of that group have gone on to do other things well outside the field of forecasting, realising (before me) the inherent difficulties in doing such a crazy job. I was a newly employed junior economist and helped my boss to produce the forecast for UK imports. Certainly at the time I seemed to be very busy. But it is difficult to remember why, although the data were input by hand, the model took at least a couple of hours to solve and we spent a lot of time and effort estimating (poorly fitting) equations and worrying about special factors, such as dock strikes, and so on.

By contrast, at Oxford Economic Forecasting (OEF) nowadays, one experienced person can update the full UK forecast in a day. This is partly because of sophisticated updating procedures, partly because the model solves in seconds and partly because we are not convinced that fretting over the many problems in the data significantly improves the overall forecast. Even the Treasury now produces its forecast with a very small team – and has limited the size of its model rather than expanding it. On some measures at least, this is one activity that has achieved high productivity growth in recent years!

Certainly, the way forecasts are produced has changed dramatically over this period. But the changes are much deeper and in many ways more significant than simply the time needed to produce a forecast. We now have very different views about the purpose and advantages of using an econometric model for analysis of UK prospects. In the early 1970s we really believed that a large team *and* a large model could produce better forecasts, and that was our main aim. When we re-estimated econometric equations the main purpose was to improve the forecasting performance. We rarely worried about the long-run properties of either a single equation or the model as a whole. We looked at simulations on the model but the model was never used for policy analysis or alternative scenarios without substantial modifications and manual intervention. As a result, the long-run properties of the model were often very poor.

Over time this all changed, with the theoretical foundations of the model and its long-run properties becoming key issues. So nowadays the forecast is produced quite quickly, but the model is used extensively to look at alternative scenarios and examine the risks surrounding any particular forecast. And at OEF, since the UK model is now part of a large multi-country system, these scenarios can cover a much wider range of issues than was possible in the 1970s. I illustrate below some of the insights that structural econometric models can provide in considering issues such as the Asian crisis, the falls in stock markets in 2001–2, and the implications of implementing Kyoto-style energy policies.

Why is forecasting so difficult?

Lord Burns, in a recent article,[2] suggests that, despite all the improvements in econometrics, computers, data manipulation and so on, there has been very little progress in reducing the size of forecast errors over the past 30 years, mainly because the world is a more complex place. It is certainly true that forecasting was always difficult and that complexity is central to that difficulty. An economy is a complex system that we do not fully understand; and it is not an isolated system. It is subject to shocks from the rest of the world or because of policy or other domestic changes.

But there is another difficulty. Participants learn from past failures. Governments, companies and individuals all remember past errors and alter their behaviour as a result. It is not surprising, then, that economic forecasters get things wrong regularly. Forecasters need to accept that they are engaged in an activity that is necessarily inaccurate to some degree!

Their difficulties have not been made easier by past suggestions by many that models would result in large improvements in forecast accuracy. So expectations of what could be achieved were often raised far too high. Cynicism has now understandably set in.

While errors in forecasting are inevitable, we in the profession have made things worse in my view by not learning all we could from our own past mistakes and thus making life even more difficult. In the next section some examples of this are spelt out in detail.

Some examples of forecasting errors

Michael Clements and David Hendry[3] set out nine possible sources of forecast error in econometric modelling systems:

- shifts in the coefficients on deterministic terms
- shifts in the coefficients on stochastic terms
- mis-specification of deterministic terms
- mis-specification of stochastic terms
- mis-estimation of the coefficients on deterministic terms
- mis-estimation of the coefficients on stochastic terms
- mis-measurement of the data
- changes in the variances of the errors
- errors cumulating over the forecast horizon

They argue that the first is the most pernicious, often causing large and systemic forecast failure. On the other hand, even large shifts in the coefficients on stochastic variables, the second source of error, have little effect on resulting forecast errors. This certainly fits my experience! Hendry and Ericsson[4] suggest that many of these deterministic shifts arise from 'things that we don't know we don't know' and propose methods for modifying models and forecasting processes to allow for this. These methods include regular re-estimation of equations and procedures for setting add-factors (residuals). In the USA frequent re-estimation is common, and in the UK careful setting of add-factors is widely followed. However, a systematic introduction of such procedures could well lead to improvements in forecasts, and certainly in their interpretation.

But while changes along these lines would be important, they would in my view not eliminate systemic forecast errors. Model users would often want to override such procedures *because* in their judgement they do have some understanding about what is happening and what this implies for the forecast. I think it is right that forecasters should try to do this but they should be clear about what they are doing and careful not to go too far. That is, we need to be very careful to distinguish between what we think we know and what we actually know. Let me illustrate by two or three recent examples.

UK consumption in the late 1980s
Financial deregulation in the early 1980s allowed UK consumers to take on more debt. This they duly did, pushing up house prices and spending more on goods and services. Certainly by 1987 this structural change was known about and was causing significant errors in most forecasts. But all forecasters (myself included) still assumed that this process of taking on more debt would end or at least slow significantly in 1988. With hindsight it is obvious that there was no good reason for believing this. And in the event it did not slow at all, so that all forecasters underestimated growth in that year and the inflationary pressure this would generate. Of course, this structural change ultimately came to an end, but only because higher growth ultimately led to higher inflation and a sharp rise in interest rates. The rest, as they say, is history.

This episode clearly illustrates that sometimes forecasters do not know as much as they think they do! Nevertheless, experience of such errors should provoke more questioning of entrenched views on how the economy behaves, helping enrich the under-standing of both forecasting issues and the operation of the economies/companies being examined.

The rise in the UK exchange rate in the late 1990s
Following the UK's ejection from the ERM in 1992, sterling fell from the equivalent of DM2.95 to a low of under DM2.30. However, in 1996 it started to rise sharply and has been well above DM3.00 (or its euro equivalent) for most of the last three years. Virtually all forecasters failed to predict the rise *and*, when it had happened, they consistently predicted a sharp fall – which has not happened either (at least so far). This period coincided with a sus-tained period of weakness for the euro vis-à-vis the US dollar, and again most forecasters were always predicting a sharp recovery from the start of any forecast made during that time.

Why did forecasters do this? I think there were two reasons. First, they generally believed that the euro was significantly below its long-term equilibrium rate. Second, they generally believed that the euro would quickly return to this long-term equilibrium rate. Given the uncertainty in any calculation of long-term equi-librium, we should all have been more circumspect in regard to the first view. But even more importantly, we should have known there was no reason for the euro to start to move quickly towards that equilibrium in the short term. Again this is surely an example of forecasters thinking they knew something when they clearly should have known they did not know!

Many other examples of this type of forecasting error exist. Many bullish US forecasters fell into this trap (and extrapolative tendencies) regarding the US stock market and productivity fol-lowing the 1990s boom. Many others, ourselves included, thought that the US stock market was overvalued but mistakenly thought that any correction would occur much earlier than it finally did. A previous example of inappropriate timing was the overvaluation of the US dollar in the early 1980s – this did come to an abrupt end in 1985–6, but not before several years of failed predictions.

To be fair, we should also acknowledge that sometimes the data are the most problematic part of the forecasting process, and not forecasters' 'judgement'. The recent example of the massive revisions to the Japanese GDP estimates for early 2002 are a case in point. It is difficult for forecasters to do a good job against such a background. And sometimes events will represent such a break from the past that there is no 'smooth' transition for forecasts that incorporate them: the UK's departure from the ERM may have been one such event (viewed from 1991 and early 1992, say), and the more recent regime shift in Argentina may be another (with the authorities reneging on the peso's US dollar peg). These cases are most likely treated as alternative 'scenarios' for this reason.

Nevertheless, I would argue that many examples can be found to suggest that forecasting errors often arise from economists thinking they know something when all the evidence suggests that they do not, especially about the speed of any move back to some sort of equilibrium.

Does this imply that forecasters should in no circumstances impose their judgement on the forecast? In my view, no. The great value of economists is that they have views – and especially on critical issues such as the long-run level of the exchange rate and the long-run value of equity markets. However, we should be upfront about the uncertainties surrounding such judgements and about when we think any equilibrium will be reached. This would suggest that the best approach would be a mixture of the statistical approach à la Hendry and the economic judgement often followed by economists. We certainly hope to incorporate such systems into the forecasting methods at OEF. This would imply that the best practice for coping with such problems is being more open to dif-ferent opinions on both the forecast and the underlying economic process generating the results. This is where more time needs to be spent (rather than on enlarging country models or fretting over retesting of the bulk of model equations).

The other important use of forecasting models

There is an implicit assumption in much of the commentary on forecasting models that their main or sole purpose is to produce forecasts. In my view, this is incorrect. Macro-econometric models provide a useful framework for making forecasts and, with current technology, it is almost as easy to produce a forecast with a 500-equation model as it is with a spreadsheet – or even the famous back of an envelope! But the big advantage of a structural macro-econometric model is that it allows the user to carry out simulations of the likely impact of changes to key assumptions built into a central forecast. Governments and corporations are just as interested in the impact of these changes as they are in the central forecast – indeed, some institutions are a lot more concerned about the scenario variants and risks than they are about point forecasts. Again, let me give a number of examples.

In 1997–8 there was a sharp fall in exchange rates and financial markets in a number of Asian economies. Initial assessments suggested that the effects would be relatively limited. However, because of the importance of trade for many of the countries in Asia, especially with the other economies in the region, and of other channels of contagion, the effects of the crisis on GDP were much bigger than first thought. A model would have clearly shown this.

Likewise, once the scale of the crisis was evident, many worried that it would lead to a sharp slowdown in the West. But simulations carried out on most models suggested that the effect on the USA and Europe of these events would be relatively small – partly because exports to Asia are only a small proportion of their GDP, and partly because of likely policy reactions in the developed economies. Many commentators found these results hard to believe, but in the event they were pretty close to the truth.

In 2000 and 2001, stock markets across the developed world fell sharply with the ending of the 'dot.com' and telecommunications bubble. Again, many predicted dire consequences for consumer spending because of negative wealth effects. However, many macro-econometric models suggested that these effects would not be that large and would be offset by rising housing wealth and lower interest rates. These same models suggested that investment might well be a greater cause for concern. Both these predictions, at least up until now, seem to be quite well supported by events.

Models can also be used to analyse the implications of policy measures such as limiting greenhouse gas emissions – the so-called Kyoto accords. These require a number of countries to cut their emissions of greenhouse gases to 1990 levels over the next ten years. To some extent this could be achieved by switching from coal to gas and by increased production of electricity from renewable sources such as wind. However, in many countries planned cuts in nuclear energy may mean that further measures will be necessary to curb demand for both electricity and gasoline if Kyoto-style targets are to be met. Carbon taxes are one of the ways to do this, with the tax revenues being used to cut budget deficits and/or reduce other taxes on consumers or companies. When one considers that such tax changes can affect competitiveness and trade for all countries – both those attempting to cut emissions and those outside the scheme – and that international trading of emission permits is an option, the need for careful modelling of all the possibilities is clear. These are not easy estimates to produce on the back of an envelope! However, in many countries this modelling has not been carried out, in some cases leading to muddled thinking and possibly inappropriate policies.

Concluding remarks

I have argued that many organisations need to make forecasts and that it is now relatively easy to use structural macro-econometric models to produce such forecasts. These models provide a framework for incorporating current theoretical knowledge. And if we are clear about what we know and do not know then procedures using the techniques coming out of the work by Hendry are available to at least reduce the risk of systemic forecasting failure. But forecasting is difficult, so we should still not expect too much. In any case, models are still very useful for analysing policy changes and assessing risks.

So the future for forecasting is reasonably bright. Just as we all listen to the weather forecasts however much we joke about their reliability, so we need economic forecasts even if the profession is rightly treated with scepticism most of the time!

Notes

1   Chairman, Oxford Economic Forecasting.
2   T. J. Burns, 'The Costs of Forecast Errors', in D. F. Hendry and N. R. Ericsson (eds), *Understanding Economic Forecasting*, MIT Press, Cambridge, MA, 2001.
3   M. Clements and D. F. Hendry, *Forecasting Non-Stationary Economic Time Series*, MIT Press, Cambridge, MA, 1999.
4   Hendry and Ericsson, op. cit., Epilogue.

11

THE BUSINESS ECONOMIST
IN STRATEGIC PLANNING

R. D. Freeman [1]

As John Kay noted in the opening of *The Business of Economics*,[2] most business executives think economics is about economic forecasting. Many business economists are of the same view. But such impressions are wide of the mark, as survey evidence from the Society of Business Economists has shown.[3] While over half of SBE members are involved in forecasting economic and market developments, other activities feature strongly in what business economists do. In fact, direct involvement in strategic planning and related aspects is about as important a function as forecasting of one type or another. It is probably more so when the 'forecasting' component of strategic planning is taken into account.

Moreover, the vast majority of companies not employing economists often use their services through engaging consultants to assist in strategy formulation. Increasingly, larger companies are turning to general consulting firms or to specialist economics consultants for strategic advice.

Interviews with business economists about their role in strategic planning show that the concept of strategic planning varies widely from company to company and from industry to industry. It ranges from three-year 'road maps' of geographical and product portfolios to detailed five- and ten-year plans for growth and profitability. Financial planning at both the business and corporate level also falls within the ambit of strategy. In many cases planning is company specific. In others it concerns mainly changes within an evolving business environment and corporate responses to those changes.

Generally, business economists working in companies and involved in strategic planning will be part of a team under a senior manager or director responsible for planning, and who, in financial services, is sometimes also the chief economist. When not part of the planning group, economists typically report to the treasurer or finance director.

Mostly it is the senior economists who take an active part in strategic planning. Typically, as people move up the ladder, their involvement in strategic issues increases, but there are no hard and fast rules. Rather there is a wide variety of experiences. Nevertheless, there are common features across industry, services, utilities and consultancies, and these are explored in the rest of this chapter.

The economic environment

Businesses plan for the future and, not surprisingly, the main input of business economists into strategic planning involves constructing a view of the future economic environment for the business for up to twenty years ahead. While there is an element of econometric forecasting in this, the main planning activities revolve very much around common-sense projections. For plans of up to three years ahead, the general practice is to use in-house forecasting models, but increasingly companies are using forecasts provided by specialist firms.

The most usual parameters provided by economists are the growth of real GDP,[4] which is seen as the best single indicator of the future scope for business activities, and a small number of other economic parameters relevant to the industry or business concerned. GDP may be of the world, of the OECD[5] area or country specific. At the corporate level, the more important economic parameters are consumers' expenditure, inflation and interest rates. For individual businesses, projections of the economic magnitudes affecting key products and demand for them are the main planning components.

For most strategic planning purposes, economists have for a long time used simple statistics, such as trend rates of growth over five-year periods of the main components of interest to their companies. Adjustments to trend rates, derived from specific studies and judgements, are frequently made to take account of major shocks, such as the two oil crises, but almost without exception economists have not had the audacity to place their faith in forecasts of longer-term growth based on sophisticated econometric models. Margins of error in modelling proved after the 1973 oil crisis to be too great, and there is no need in planning terms to spend a huge amount of time and resources looking for accuracy that is not to be realised. With the break in trend after 1973, for example, the average annual growth rate of OECD GDP has been remarkably stable at around 2.5 per cent. With appropriate adjustments, projections of trend growth rates for both world and OECD GDP have been more than adequate to meet most planning needs for a broad view of the economic environment.

Given this background, it is tempting to argue that there really is no need for economists to be involved in setting the parameters of corporate strategies. After all, getting hold of trend rates of growth does not require great skills. If only life were so simple. Even with this type of approach to formulating the basic framework of strategy, there is an important role for the economist in determining what would be appropriate adjustments for the next five years compared with the last five or ten. For example, looking back, should companies have made any changes to their planning assumptions and strategies in the early 1990s to take account of the so-called peace dividend? What will be the impact in the first decade of the 21st century of the 'new' economy? These types of questions are endless, and they are questions economists, because of their experience, are best suited to answer.

Again, planners are often tempted to put the best possible gloss on events and to make planning assumptions that inevitably turn out to be far too optimistic. Economists, because of their understanding of the data and of forecasting techniques, are less prone to this. All the economists interviewed for this chapter said that they continually battled with their non-economist colleagues to adopt sensible rather than 'hockey stick' planning assumptions so loved by businessmen. As well as contributing to reality, the economist has another important function, which is to ensure consistency in the broad planning assumptions across both the individual components and regions and countries. Consistency may sound easy to achieve but it is not so without the necessary training and knowledge of economic statistics and national accounts.

Within the overall growth of the world economy, regional and country details are also critical for many companies. Where this is so, global parameters need to be broken down geographically. Again, trend rates of growth are helpful, but much more judgement is required by economists in projecting growth paths of individual countries than for the world economy. This is because national growth rates tend to fluctuate more over typical planning periods than the global aggregates. While annual average GDP growth rates in the United States have not varied greatly between longer-term periods over the last 30 years, there have been major changes in trend growth rates in the other G7 countries, most notably in the United Kingdom. The fluctuations in longer-term performance of many of the smaller OECD countries have also been substantial, as have those in most non-OECD countries.

Assessing the factors influencing longer-term national growth rates falls clearly within the economist's bailiwick. The answers can and have had a large impact on strategic decisions. In association mainly with projections of cost, prices and exchange rates, growth projections have been central to global investment decisions throughout the corporate sector. As overseas investment by many companies increasingly replaced trade as the main driver of globalisation, decisions about where to site overseas facilities have been a critical aspect of strategy. This is well illustrated by the step change in investment by British manufacturing and service companies in the United States from the early 1970s, and then into Continental Europe in the 1980s. In the 1990s, Asia Pacific became a strong magnet for direct investment.

In the last 50 years, the challenges to business economists in setting the economic framework for strategy have been manifold and large. Among them, several stand out. The impact of the oil crises and the effect of North Sea oil were at the forefront in the 1970s, as was membership of the EEC. The 1980s saw the economic consequences of Mrs Thatcher, monetarism, Black Monday and European 'sclerosis'. Then came the Single Market, EMU and, most recently, the euro and the 'new' economy. Throughout the period, the future of sterling has been a constant poser for economists.

Just as detailed strategies are never set in concrete because of changes in the business environment or corporate mistakes, so the tasks of the economist are not over once the strategic economic parameters are agreed at the appropriate level – usually the board. Most planning processes are continuous. It is common practice for companies to review and update their strategic planning framework each year or every two years in conjunction with their budget cycle. Strategies may be reworked every three years, but more frequent adaptation within strategies and updating of economic projections is normal. A broad statement of strategy – for example, raising the percentage of sales outside the United Kingdom from 30 per cent to 60 per cent within five years – may well hold good for five years, but events can readily bring about changes in the ways the strategy is pursued.

Monitoring developments in the economy to support these re-assessments of projections is a continuing task for the economist involved in strategic planning. In addition, as businesses develop new proposals and projects, up-to-date and more specific planning assumptions are required, and they have to be assumptions that are consistent with the broader projections being used throughout the company. In this aspect of their work, and in conjunction with annual budgets, economists are often asked to assess the probabilities of particular prospects and the sensitivities relating to some key business relationship. What, for example, are the probabilities of real GDP in the OECD area or the United Kingdom growing by 1.5, 2 or 2.5 per cent a year on average over the next five years? As regards sensitivities for the economy, issues might well be what are the effects on GDP of every 5 per cent increase in the price of North Sea oil or of each 5 per cent change in the effective exchange rate? Or what effect will each half percentage point change in the growth of OECD GDP have on corporate profits? The list is never ending, and probabilities and sensitivities also play a part in planning at the business or industry level.

Country risk analysis

The question of country risk is often closely associated with analysis of the economy as part of the economist's role in strategic planning. This is especially pronounced in banking but it also applies to other services and manufacturing.

Risk analysis is seen in many companies as the key driver of any strategy for the expansion of operations outside the UK. This aspect of the economist's input into strategic planning has increased considerably over the last twenty years with the advance of globalisation. Generally, economists are asked for five-year assessments of the main economic risks of investing either in financial assets or manufacturing plants in selected countries.

For some economists in the financial sector, country risk is their chief concern. Constant monitoring of countries judged to be high and medium risk enables economists to contribute to evolving strategies. The main economic parameters of interest in this area are inflationary prospects, exchange rates, international debt and the likelihood of default. Close attention is paid to information and studies from the IMF, the World Bank and the Economist

Intelligence Unit. Sometimes, specialist risk consultancies are used to supplement the economic analysis with information about political risk.

The contribution of country risk analysis to strategic thinking is best illustrated by three examples where there has been a considerable influence on strategy. The first relates to the 1997–8 Asian crisis which led to marked changes in strategy of some major British firms in the region. In the banking sector, risk analysis resulted in some banks reducing substantially their credit exposures in Indonesia and a curtailment of longer-term investments in other Asian countries. The second example is also from the financial sector, where risk analysis resulted in at least two British banks limiting their strategic exposures in Argentina before the peso link with the dollar was recently broken. The third example is from manufacturing. In the first half of the 1990s, a large British company decided to reduce its strategic drive into Japan following an analysis by its economists of the risks of a banking crisis in that country.

Project and market planning

Risk and probability analysis by economists extends in many instances from countries to individual projects both on a continuing and an ad hoc basis. Frequently an important input into this aspect of planning is the assessment of the rounds of negotiations relating to world trade arrangements, formerly under the auspices of GATT[6] and now the WTO.[7] How, for instance, will the Uruguay Round proposals affect particular projects such as the siting of a manufacturing plant in a G7 country versus a developing country? For technology companies, the impact of the TRIPS agreement[8] continues to be of strategic significance. A key strategic question for economists in banks and other financial institutions to answer is how changing international financial regulations could affect investment strategies in competing financial products.

Economists are regularly asked within a strategic context to review the prospects for individual product markets and how, if at all, market structures could change within the timescale of corporate strategies. Such projects may partly impinge on market research but they remain very much the property of the economist either as project leader or as part of a multi-disciplinary team. On occasions, strategic projects are triggered by outside events such as Black Monday, the fall of the Berlin Wall or 11 September. On other occasions they arise out of strategic reviews aimed at raising performance.

In the former category, the two oil crises and later environmental concerns about greenhouse gases have long occupied economists in the transport and energy sectors. Specific projects have included the impact of oil-price changes on the structure of the car market, focusing on large versus small cars and car mileages. Also in the energy sector, privatisation of the electricity and gas markets and the way they are regulated have absorbed a great deal of analytical effort which has had important consequences for investment decisions. The prospect of the Single Market and its advent in 1992 also initiated many strategic projects relating to market growth and structures and how they might change as trade barriers came down. A more recent example comes from the hotel industry, where an analysis of hotel occupancy rates in the USA before and after 11 September resulted in a revised investment strategy.

Projects arising from regular strategic reviews mostly do not get the attention given to projects triggered by external shocks. They are, however, more frequent and more important for strategies. External shocks seem to loom much larger in the minds of executives than they should, and in the short term they create much more excitement in boardrooms than run-of-the-mill strategy reviews before they are brought to earth by economists and subsequently by events. Many strategies have failed to deliver because boards have greatly overestimated the likely effects of external shocks on their businesses. It seems hard for those who are not economists to learn that the effects of external shocks are never as great as they stubbornly believe. A similar problem in the 1980s and part of the 1990s was trying to convince directors that the business cycle still existed.

Mostly review-based projects are about the future developments in specific product markets or the wider markets that companies supply. Mostly, too, the projects form the basis of discussions about product portfolios and corporate structures. There are many examples where economists have contributed significantly to major strategic changes in large British companies. Thus, as a result of a study by its economists in the mid-1990s, one bank made a strategic shift into wholesale operations to reduce reliance on retail banking. Earlier in the 1990s, as a result of a strategic review by its chief economist, a manufacturing company with subsidiaries in about 30 countries which operated independently brought them together under a single umbrella prior to exiting the business altogether. In agriculture, a similar study saw the beginning of increased concentration of suppliers to the industry in the mid-1990s, which is continuing.

Many industries, not only in the UK but in all the G7 countries, have experienced increased concentration as companies have restructured in their attempts to enhance shareholder value. Not infrequently, strategic aspirations to gain market share and power through mergers and acquisitions have been dashed by competition considerations. Often proposals for strategic alliances never get off the starting blocks because of the economist's analyses of the likely competitive effects. The importance of the economics of competition for strategies has almost certainly increased during the last decade, with leading companies turning for advice to their economists, if they employed them, and increasingly to consulting firms.

Scenarios

Finally, there are strategic scenarios to which business economists often contribute. The number of companies formally using scenarios in their planning is relatively small but they still have a significant place in strategy development. Increasingly, too, companies are buying in scenario services from consultants rather than devoting internal resources to them.

The nature of scenarios varies widely between companies, as does their use in strategic planning. Shell is the company best known in this area, employing a full-time team of twelve, including two economists, to develop them. The head of the team is a trained economist. In addition to their own economists, Shell uses an economic consultancy to develop the economic input to the scenarios. Shell has two current scenarios of global developments looking twenty years ahead. They are presented regularly to Shell's businesses around the world with the aim of stimulating strategic thinking. As such, the scenarios are not part of the formal planning process but they make an important contribution to the ideas-forming strategy.

While a small number of other companies use global scenarios with twenty-year horizons to help develop strategy, they are best described as 'informal' and, again, are not usually built into strategic plans. The more usual practice is to use ten-year scenarios to test the robustness of strategies under different patterns of development of the world economy. Another variant employed in ICI until the mid-1990s was for directors to decide which scenario from several prepared by the economists the company and ICI's businesses would use as the basis of their strategic planning. The other scenarios were used to test the sensitivities of strategy and projects to alternative world developments. In these exercises, the main economic parameters were GDP, industrial production, inflation and exchange rates. The ICI approach ensured consistency across all the businesses. In the absence of large shocks, the scenarios were fully reworked about every two years. But whatever the approach of different companies, scenarios are seen generally as an effective way not only of stimulating thinking about the future but also of identifying risks to strategies.

The business economist's tool kit

The business economist's training and experience can add a great deal to the professionalism of strategic planning, and there is ample evidence that SBE members have done so over the last 50 years. Economists can provide a high level of analytical skills not available from other disciplines by applying the tools acquired during their education and experience in the workplace. This tool kit embraces a knowledge and understanding of theories about the working of the economy, of the statistical sources for economic information and of the methods for analysing those data.

The tools economists bring to strategic planning cover a wide range of economics. Undoubtedly, the most widely used is the knowledge of national accounts and general macroeconomic theory, including international trade theory. Together they form the basis of the many macroeconomic models used by companies in their long-term growth projections and scenario building. They are also the principal assets of the consultants on whom many companies rely for their strategic frameworks. In the financial sector, a firm grasp of monetary theory and its evolution is clearly at the top of the list. A general knowledge of monetary theory and the interpretation of how it affects markets is also necessary in other sectors. Associated with monetary theory, the latest thinking on how foreign exchange markets work ranks highly in the kit of many business economists.

As would be expected, the microeconomic tools used by business economists are more diverse than those on the macro side. The list below is by no means exhaustive, but it gives an idea of the most frequently used tools in microeconomic analysis. The theory of the firm and industrial organisation theory are the basis of much of this work in most business sectors, as are price theory and production economics. Other tools in the kit include game theory, the economics of regulation, valuation theory and project evaluation techniques. Competition analysis is growing in importance, along with the economics of the environment. Econometrics is widely employed in microeconomic analysis and an understanding of it is necessary to keep abreast of the latest thinking in the discipline.

To some extent, the tool kit enables the economist to limit the potential dangers from the use of casually acquired economic ideas when formulating strategies. Reference has already been made to 'hockey stick' planning and over-optimism about the disappearance of the business cycle. All those interviewed for this chapter have experienced such DIY economics to a greater or lesser degree, and the majority consider overcoming its excesses and bringing balance and reality to strategic planning an essential part of their jobs.

Concluding remarks

When the SBE was founded 50 years ago, strategic planning was far less sophisticated and professional than it is now. For large numbers of companies, the perceived need for detailed strategies was small. Despite foreign exchange restrictions, resource restrictions of various types and difficult labour relations, corporate life was relatively comfortable. Growth was reasonable, inflation low, competitive pressures were non-existent or weak in most markets, and demand was strong, even though some empire markets were being lost. Trade barriers offered worthwhile protection and the boom in foreign direct investment was in its infancy. Shareholders were quiescent and companies were spared the need to be forever looking over their shoulders at City institutions.

The huge transformation in the business environment during the lifetime of the SBE has itself revolutionised approaches to corporate planning. The main features of the transformation are many and varied, but among the more important are probably the acceleration in the pace of change in most markets as a result of the reduction in tariffs and restrictions on capital movements, the emergence of increasingly strong competitive conditions in most industries, the growth in foreign investment, stronger financial market pressures, the information revolution, and the spread of global markets.

The increase in uncertainty in business life associated with all these changes has raised substantially over time the importance of strategic planning and has improved the way it is carried out. These improvements have been aided and abetted by the growth in business schools and the growing numbers of MBAs entering business, but they have also increased the demand for the services of economists to bring their tool kit to bear on the complex analytical issues involved in strategic planning. Members of the SBE in all sectors of business have contributed in many different and important ways to the conduct of strategic planning in a wide range of British companies. The opportunities for economists in planning are probably greater now than at any time over the last 50 years, and the demand for their tool kit greater than ever.

Notes

1   Richard Freeman is a consulting economist and was formerly Chief Economist at ICI.

2   J. A. Kay, *The Business of Economics*, Oxford University Press, 1996.

3   J. Leyland, 'Where Economists Work', *Business Economist*, vol. 28, no. 1, SBE, 1997.

4   Gross Domestic Product measures the value of total output in an economy. Real GDP measures changes in this total value excluding the effect of changes in the general level of prices. See Note 3, Chapter 1 – *Ed*.

5   See Note 2, Chapter 1 – *Ed*.

6   General Agreement on Trade and Tariffs.

7   World Trade Organisation.

8   The Trade in Intellectual Property Agreement was made as part of the Uruguay Round of trade negotiations.

12

ECONOMICS, BUSINESS STRATEGY AND RICARDIAN RENT

John Kay[1]

Most business people think that economics is macroeconomic forecasting. They are not impressed with the results of such forecasting, although they continue to think they need it, and as a result they hold economists in low esteem. They have also come to see this activity as increasingly dispensable, which is why, outside the financial services sector, the role of economists in business has been in decline.

Yet only a very small proportion of academic economists are engaged in macroeconomic forecasting, or undertake research on issues related to it. And these questions also play a relatively minor role in economics education. Perhaps too minor – today you encounter economics graduates who have no knowledge or experience of the contents and concepts of national economic statistics. But most research in economics today focuses on microeconomic issues. The principal research themes of the last 30 years include non-cooperative game theory models of industrial organisation, principal-agent models and associated analyses of contracts and incentives, and the economics of markets with imperfect information. All these subjects are concerned with issues more directly relevant than overall macroeconomic trends to the questions that businesses manage on a day-to-day basis. Cost and pricing strategies, incentive structures and competitor reactions are the stuff of everyday business thinking, and most business people would much prefer to devote resources to a better understanding of these issues than to receive even accurate knowledge of the future path of interest rates or national income. But this recent work by economists has made very little impact on business.

The role that economics might have played has been filled by business strategy. The subject of strategy came into being in the 1960s. Business schools and consultants sought an integrative framework that would bring together fields as disparate as finance theory and organisational behaviour. And large-scale planning exercises were fashionable at national, corporate and business unit levels. The potentially revolutionary impact of information technology was becoming apparent, and people seriously imagined that one day both national economies and individual businesses might be run by computers. This was the era in which Robert McNamara took the skills of the planner from the Ford Motor Company to the Department of Defense and then to the World Bank, and General Electric vied with the Soviet Union to create the most developed systems of centralised strategic control of diverse business activities. The leading British journal in business strategy was established with the title *Long Range Planning*. It seems a long time ago.

The role of economists in these planning processes was limited to the provision of macroeconomic input (and, rather oddly, to the development of some of the mathematical programming techniques that were used). The intermediate area – the scope and functions of business itself – was off limits. In the words of H. E. Ansoff, one of the founders of the new subject of strategy: 'Study of the firm has been the long time concern of the economics profession. Unfortunately for our present purpose, the so-called microeconomic theory of the firm which occupies much of the economists' thought and attention, sheds relatively little light on decision-making processes in a real world firm.'[2]

And economists of the time would not have disagreed. Industrial economics in the 1960s was dominated by what was then
called the Structure-Conduct-Performance paradigm, empirical in
approach, but eschewing the issues that preoccupied business
strategists. Joe Bain, leader of the Structure-Conduct-Performance school, defined its scope.

> I am concerned with the environmental setting within which enter-
> prises operate and in how they behave in these settings as producers,
> sellers and buyers. By contrast, I do not take an internal approach,
> more appropriate to the field of management science, such as could
> inquire how enterprises do and should behave in ordering their inter-
> nal operations and would attempt to instruct them accordingly ... my
> primary unit for analysis is the industry or competing groups of firms,
> rather than the individual firm or the economy wide aggregate of
> enterprises.[3]

A definitive account of the S-C-P approach is found in
Scherer's textbook,[4] where his defining framework makes his concerns clear.

The analysis runs from basic conditions of supply and demand
through market structure to conduct and performance. Within this
framework, there can be no answer to the central question of business strategy – why does one firm do better than another in the
same environment? All face the same conditions of supply and
demand, all operate within the same market structure: all should
therefore engage in the same conduct and produce the same performance.

But what does Scherer mean by 'performance'? Not profit,
growth or market share – the routine concerns of corporate executives. Scherer's criteria of performance are 'production and
allocative efficiency, progress, full employment, and equity'.
These are the issues of public policy, not business policy. Scherer
and his colleagues had an influence on business through the application of their framework to issues of anti-trust and regulation, not

Figure 2 **A model of industrial analysis**

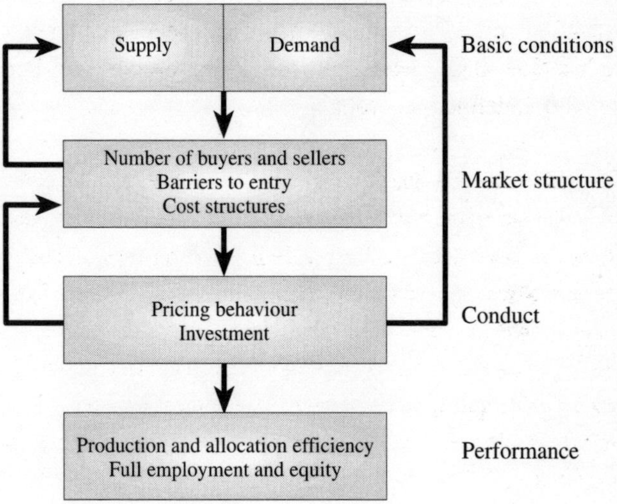

Source: Simplified from Scherer (1980).

through its use by business people themselves. The curious consequences of this continue to the present day. Economics continues to provide the framework for public policy towards business, while having very little influence on business policy itself.

Porter's competitive strategy

An early and celebrated attempt to give business strategy greater economic content is found in Michael Porter's *Competitive Strategy*.[5] Porter took the Structure-Conduct-Performance paradigm and expressed it in more business-friendly terms. The resemblance between Scherer's framework – in which basic conditions of supply and demand determine market structure and firm behaviour – and Porter's 'five forces' is immediately obvious.

And it is not accidental. Porter earned his PhD in the Harvard

Figure 3 **The five forces**

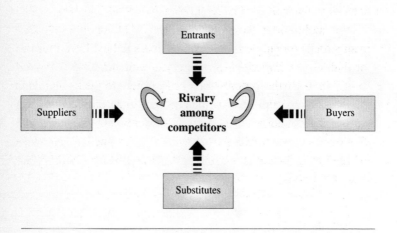

Source: Based on Porter (1985).

Economics Department – the world centre for research in the Structure-Conduct-Performance paradigm – and then crossed the Charles river to describe that paradigm to the students of the Harvard Business School.

Porter's work enjoyed great success and received much attention both in the business-school world and in business itself. This success demonstrated the hunger in parts of the business world for a more analytic framework for strategic issues. Yet the reasons why the S-C-P approach had not provided that analytic framework in the 1960s continued to limit the relevance of the insights it could provide. S-C-P focuses on the structure of the industry rather than the behaviour of the firm or the interrelationship between the firm and its environment. Since all businesses in the same market encounter the same five forces, why do some do well and others badly? This is the question that Bain had explicitly declined to answer, and Porter's framework did not – could not – fill the gap. Porter's second book, *Competitive Advantage*,[6] seeks to meet that deficiency, and in it one can see a recognition that the 'new industrial organisation' might have a role to play. But this is potential, not realisation, and the most important influence of the book has been its analysis of vertical relationships (the value chain).

Nor could Porter escape from the Harvard Economics Department's focus on public rather than business policy. If you turn to the index of *Competitive Strategy* you will not find the word 'profit' in it. By the 1990s, Porter had reverted to the economist's traditional preoccupation, and had become more commentator on current affairs than business guru. His most recent major work is *The Competitive Advantage of Nations*,[7] designed to compare international economic performance and prescribe appropriate industrial policies.

Economic rents

Porter's work was therefore ultimately unsuccessful in providing an economic basis for business strategy. But there is a concept linking business strategy and industrial economics: it is the concept of economic rent. The conduct of business is principally driven by the creation, exploitation and defence of economic rents. The search for economic rents defines the horizontal and vertical boundaries of the firm, and with that the structure of industries. Changes in that structure follow from changes in the nature or availability of the factors that give rise to rents. Scarce factors, unique history and capabilities characterised by uncertain imitability are the principal sources of rent.

The terminology is unfortunate. For most people, rent is what you have to pay if you don't own your house. The inapt term reflects the long history of the concept: when David Ricardo first expounded the theory of rent two centuries ago, agriculture was still the most important form of economic activity and landlord and tenant was its characteristic form of organisation. The consultants Stern Stewart have recently enjoyed some success in promoting the measurement of rent under the title 'economic value added': but the term value added is already used by economists to mean something

Figure 4 **Ricardian rent versus firm rent**

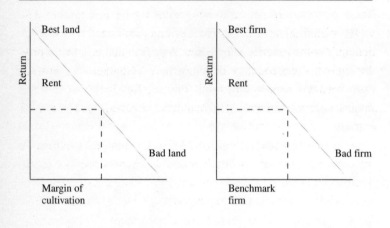

quite different. After failing to persuade people to talk of added value, I have reached the conclusion that the best course is to use the phrase 'economic rent', and provide the explanation.

That explanation is illuminating in its own right. Ricardo's famous analysis involved an ordering of land in England from best to worst.

The price of corn determined the margin of cultivation. Land at the margin of cultivation was barely worth bringing into use and would earn no rent. The higher the price of corn, the more extensive was the margin of cultivation. Land inside the margin of cultivation – better and therefore intramarginal land – would command progressively higher rents. The rent of any cultivated territory would be equal to the degree of its superiority over land at the margin of cultivation.

Firms in a market may be arranged in exactly the same way. The margin of cultivation now corresponds to the point at which firms just earn the cost of capital, and hence find it worthwhile to remain in business. Better firms – intramarginal firms – earn higher returns, either through lower costs or higher returns per unit of expenditure, and so earn rents. And any market has firms outside the commercial equivalent of the margin of cultivation – businesses that are not currently producing for that market, but which would do so if the product price or anticipated growth in demand for the product were higher. Any firm that is actually producing earns rent equal to its competitive advantage – the difference between revenues per unit of cost for that firm and the revenue per unit of cost that could be obtained by a potential entrant.

Why are intramarginal firms able to earn returns in excess of the cost of capital? In Ricardo's account, this was because good-quality land was in scarce supply, and the answer is essentially the same when this framework is applied to modern business. Businesses earn rent because they enjoy access to scarce factors which cannot be reproduced by marginal firms. If they are to develop sustainable advantages, and continue to earn rents, it is necessary that these scarce factors not be reproduced by marginal firms even after they understand the benefits that accrue to the initiating, intramarginal firms.

Sometimes the scarce factors that give intramarginal firms their distinctive capabilities are more or less precisely analogous to Ricardo's superior land – as when oil or mineral companies enjoy exclusive access to particular scarce resources, or pharmaceutical companies and music publishers hold valuable patents or copyrights. Other strategic assets may be established through private action, as when Microsoft leverages its dominance of the operating systems market to establish dominance in browsers.

More often, however, scarce factors reside in structures of relationships. Brands and reputations are common distinctive capabilities which reflect established relationships with customers. Distinctive supplier architecture and structures of relationships within the business itself are other frequently encountered types of distinctive capability. You can never exactly replicate the history of a business, and many distinctive capabilities – particularly reputations and supplier relationships – are established in this way. Uncertain imitability provides another opportunity for distinctiveness. No one – including the firm itself – can precisely define those elements of its internal routines which contribute to the effectiveness of its performance. The power of such routines is the result of their tacit nature. If they could be defined precisely, they could be written down, they could be copied, and they would no longer be likely to generate rents for the businesses that hold them.

Innovations provide opportunities to establish distinctive capabilities but, in most industries, innovations are readily imitable if they are successful. This process, by which innovation yields transitory rents which are rapidly eliminated through adoption by other firms, is a central dynamic of a capitalist economy. But innovation is a source of sustainable rents only in those relatively few industries – such as pharmaceuticals – in which patent protection, or process secrecy, is effective. More often, companies that base their success on innovation do so as a result of an internal architecture that enables them to generate an extended series of innovations, or a reputation with customers which attracts buyers to an innovative company or secures ready acceptance of the product and process innovations which that business generates.

Economic rents and the theory of the firm

From Marshall through Bain, the focus of attention of economists was, as I have described, on the industry as the unit of business analysis. A corollary of this was that little attention was given to theories of the firm. Given that the rise of the large corporation was probably the single most important economic development of the twentieth century, this omission was serious. Businesses were described as technologies, equipped with a production function. The absence of a theory of the firm in economics was a potent illustration, and cause, of the divorce between macroeconomic theory and business strategy.

This exaggerates. There were theories of the firm. The most

important and influential of these was advanced by Donald Coase, who was eventually to become one of the select handful of British economists to win the Nobel Prize for this work.[8] But the Coaseian perspective on the firm, in which the boundaries of the firm are determined by the balance between the costs of internal organisation through hierarchical processes and the different costs of external transactions mediated through the market, does not help much in assessing a company's market position and strategic opportunities. It does raise what was to become in the 1980s a central business issue – the make/buy question, what to do in-house and what to outsource. But Coase's analysis fails to address broader questions of business strategy because, in common with the S-C-P paradigm, it cannot explain why different firms undertaking the same activities perform differently – after all, each of them confronts the same trade-off between internal and external costs.

But around the time business strategy was developed as a distinct subject, Edith Penrose founded a rather different approach to these issues in her classic *Theory of the Growth of the Firm*.[9] The essence of Penrose's approach was to see the firm as a collection of capabilities. Different firms in the same industry consist of different collections of capabilities. Both the boundaries of the firm, and the relative performance of businesses in the same market, are defined by the match between these capabilities and the characteristics of the market. It is the appropriateness of that match which is the key determinant of business success.

Penrose's approach, with its emphasis on capabilities, lends itself naturally to a view of the firm which emphasises its capacity to generate rents from its distinctive capabilities. But it was some time before these ideas achieved much attention from economists – Penrose's institutional bias, and modest use of mathematics, did not fit the tenor of the times. Then in the 1980s this capability-based view of the character of the firm became the resource-based theory of strategy, which is today the dominant paradigm in the academic strategy literature.

For a time, the evolutionary approach to the development of

firms, industries and markets – which had been loosely but not centrally part of economic thinking since the time of Marshall – seemed to represent a quite different tradition. It was developed more extensively in the 1980s by Nelson and Winter, and the growth of interest in evolutionary biology has led to an explosion of evolutionary models of all kinds. This conception of the development of the firm sees its expansion and transformation as a process of continuous adaptation to an external environment.

But it is now apparent that the similarities between the resource-based and evolutionary approaches are much more significant than the differences. The ability of firms to choose their capabilities is very limited. This must be so: if businesses were completely free to select their capabilities, all would focus on collections that were demonstrated to be successful. These collections would immediately cease to be distinctive and could no longer be a source of economic rents.

The answer to the question that adherents of the resource-based theory of strategy are always asked – how do I create the appropriate set of capabilities? – is that it must be hard, otherwise the process would not yield sustainable rents for those who have achieved it. Very often, perhaps usually, the successful match of capabilities to market characteristics does not come from the fine-tuning of capabilities to the requirement of the market: rather the market selects those firms which have the capabilities most relevant to requirements. This is the point at which evolutionary and resource-based theories converge. It is easy to exaggerate the influence of conscious design in the success of businesses.

Rents and finance

The economic rent earned by a firm is equal to the difference between its operating profits and the risk-adjusted cost of capital multiplied by the replacement cost of its assets used in the business. The second figure is the amount that a prospective entrant

Figure 5 The equivalence of measures of financial performance

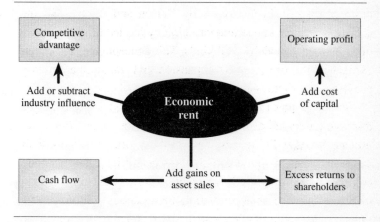

would need to earn to justify being in that business. It therefore provides the benchmark – the margin of cultivation – for the calculation of economic rents.

Financial economics rests on two basic valuation theorems. Samuelson showed that valuations are invariant to the depreciation scheme employed,[10] and Modigliani and Miller that valuations are invariant to capital structure.[11] Taken together these two theorems yield an equivalence theorem which displays the fundamental relationships between economic rents and other measures of the financial performance of a business.

Over the lifetime of the business, there is an identity between the net present value at the cost of capital of

- economic rents computed at replacement cost
- economic rents computed on a historic cost basis
- net cash flow
- excess returns to shareholders (i.e. returns in excess of the risk-adjusted cost of capital on the market value of equity)

The measurement of economic rent thus provides the link between four basic perspectives on the financial performance of the firm.

- a strategic perspective which emphasises competitive advantage
- an accounting perspective which looks at return on historic cost
- an internal investment perspective which focuses on discounted cash flow
- a capital market perspective which evaluates shareholder return

The equivalence theorem completes the link between the differential performance of firms and the profits they earn. It enables economists writing about strategy today to put profit into their index. Perhaps one day it will also enable them to put profit into their pocket.

Conclusion

Most economists continue to be uncomfortable with the idea that firms earn economic rents. The dominant tradition in economics – this certainly includes those who followed the S-C-P paradigm, but extends much more widely – regards rents as evidence of monopoly. From this perspective, it is the job of anti-trust authorities and other agencies of public policy to try to eliminate these rents. There is a sense in which all economic rents are the product of monopoly: there is something inherently monopolistic about possession of any scarce factor. But the economic rents that accrue to Beckham or Pavarotti are not the result of monopoly in the ordinary, pejorative sense in which we use that word. And nor are the economic rents that accrue to successful firms. Economic rents that are the product of trusted brands, valued reputations, innovations and distinctive structures of relationships reflect features of modern economic life which contribute, not just to the effectiveness of firms, but to the effectiveness of the market economy. Only when business economists take rents to their hearts will they

recapture the ground they abandoned 40 years ago to strategy consultants.

Notes

1   John Kay is author of *Foundations of Corporate Success* (1993),
     The Business of Economics (1996) and *The Truth about Markets*
     (2003).

2   H. E. Ansoff, *Corporate Strategy*, McGraw Hill, New York,
     1965.

3   J. S. Bain, *Industrial Organization*, pp. vii–viii, Wiley, New
     York, 1959.

4   F. M. Scherer, *Industrial Market Structure and Economic Per-
     formance*, Houghton Mifflin, Boston, MA, 1970. See also
     F. M. Scherer and D. Ross, *Industrial Market Structure and Eco-
     nomic Performance*, 2nd edn, Houghton Mifflin, 1980.

5   M. E. Porter, *Competitive Strategy*, Free Press, New York, 1980.

6   M. E. Porter, *Competitive Advantage*, Free Press, New York,
     1985.

7   M. E. Porter, *The Competitive Advantage of Nations*, Free Press,
     New York, 1990.

8   R. Coase, 'The Nature of the Firm', *Economica*, no. 4, 1937,
     pp. 386–405.

9   E. T. Penrose, *The Theory of the Growth of the Firm*, Oxford
     University Press, 1959.

10   P. A. Samuelson, 'Tax Deductibility of Economic Depreciation
     to Insure Invariant Valuation', *Journal of Political Economy*,
     vol. 72, 1964, pp. 604–66.

11   F. Modigliani and M. H. Miller, 'The Cost of Capital, Corpora-
     tion Finance and the Theory of Investment', *The American Eco-
     nomic Review*, vol. 48, no. 3, 1958, pp. 261–97.

13

FIFTY YEARS OF THE SOCIETY OF BUSINESS ECONOMISTS

Donald Anderson [1]

Foundations: 1953

London in the early months of 1953 was a somewhat grim city. World War II had ended little more than seven years previously, leaving the country impoverished. It had been followed by several years of austerity, with consumption rationed and activity oriented as far as possible towards manufactured exports. A radical government had introduced a new phase in the country's political life which was to last nearly 35 years, but the initial social revolution had been achieved at significant economic cost.

Physically, the environment was drab. Over the winter, the city had been frequently enveloped in dense smogs, the product of a heavy reliance on coal by transport, industry and households. In less affluent areas, many of the latter were still lit by gas. Television ownership was small; news was obtained from the radio and press, and entertainment from the cinema. The majority did not eat out, and for most the theatre was for special occasions. The roads, however, were relatively clear, and London Transport, with trams and trolleybuses as well as Tubes and buses (but not the renowned Routemaster – that was as yet six years away), functioned to a high standard.

Politically, economically and socially, it was a hybrid period.

The British Empire remained extensive despite the loss of India. Winston Churchill was prime minister. The balance of payments problem was persistent and severe and housing was in short supply, but unemployment and inflation were low, and the UK still had a higher GDP per head than most other European countries. The welfare state had become established and public utilities, coal and transport nationalised. The class system and the limitations it incurred were still evident, but had been much diluted by the war.

The war had left many legacies. Among them was the gradual intrusion of a new level of professionalism in certain aspects of government, industry and commerce. This professionalism brought with it the use of statistics and quantitative techniques to aid decision-taking and evolve strategies; objective intelligence systems to research markets and their trends and to analyse competitors; and the application of academic theory to real-life situations. One discipline relevant to all these approaches was that of economics. As a result, by the early 1950s economists were being employed in a professional capacity in business as well as in government and academia. Their number was small, but the business economist was emerging as an occupation.

The position of this new breed was not particularly easy. Economics was a growing discipline in academia, but its theory had become increasingly remote from reality and was frequently irrelevant to the problems of business. Published statistics were geared heavily towards the government's needs, and meaningful data could be difficult to obtain. And as communications with other professionals could be poor, particularly between organisations, the business economist had to overcome these difficulties in relative isolation.

These problems were felt more keenly in industrial companies than in other sectors, but were by and large a common experience. They proved a particular problem for those employed in consultancies, whose audiences were by definition primarily external, and whose business depended on information about the structure and behaviour of the real economy, and sufficient knowledge of its characteristics at a detailed level to be able to interpret its behaviour. One such affected was a relatively new member of the staff of the Economist Intelligence Unit, a personable young Scot, Campbell Fraser. He decided to improve the situation. With the aid of three of his own colleagues and two outsiders whom he knew to be of like mind – John Dixon of Dunlop and Clive Dalton of Esso – he set up a meeting with a view to establishing a small group of economists working in business who might gather regularly to discuss their professional problems and their work.

The meeting took place early in 1953, in the faded grandeur of the St Ermin's Hotel in Westminster. The record of the event has been lost, but the attendance list shows there to have been 33 present. Of these, thirteen were from industry, seven were from consultancies or market research organisations, three from trade associations, three from the financial sector, and one from the National Institute for Economic and Social Research. The remaining six – a fifth of the total – were from government.

The motives of those present reflected their positions. For some, the divergence between the real world and economic theory was a prime concern. As John Dixon recalled some seventeen years later, 'academic practice had become quite out of touch with business practice and we wanted to bridge the gap, with the particular aim of getting economic theory rewritten to accord more with the facts of business life'. Others, however, were more concerned with keeping in touch with developments in economic theory, accepting its increasing remoteness. A third group was more interested in exchanging views and analysing government policies and current affairs, and with developing a form of club that would facilitate the exchange of ideas and experiences, and so mitigate professional isolation. A fourth group was motivated by a perceived need for a body that could provide professional defence, both setting standards and promoting the interests of its members.

In the event, the meeting decided to set up a discussion group. It would operate without membership subscriptions.

Meetings would (at least initially) be held in a local pub, the
Four Feathers; proceedings would be off the record. A committee was elected to manage the group, composed of the remaining three instigators and Alan Smith of ICI's Intelligence
Department. Campbell Fraser was elected chairman. A rule was
established to allow no more than one participant per industry
(and therefore, in effect, one firm per industry), in order to
promote open discussion and preserve confidentiality. Although
unanimously agreed, this had the curious effect of excluding
from future meetings a number of the founding members. These
included Alan Brazier and Elwyn Jones, from Dunlop and Esso
respectively, both of whom were later to make significant contributions to the development of the group. Such people were
permitted to attend meetings as alternates if the primary
member were not able to do so, but the basic membership was,
as a result of this rule, restricted.

The group decided to call itself the Business Economics
Group. The forerunner of the Society of Business Economists had
been born.

Growth: 1953–7

The early meetings of the group – of which again there is no
written record – followed the pattern agreed at the first meeting,
although it quickly became apparent that the ideal of a subscrip-
tion-less body would not be viable. A membership fee of one
pound and ten shillings (£1.50) was therefore adopted. Almost
immediately, a need was articulated for a focus for the round
table discussions, and outside speakers were invited to attend in
order to bring specific areas of expertise to the gatherings. Some
of those invited were essentially political, such as Harold Wilson,
who had recently left the Board of Trade (following the acces-
sion of the Conservative government) and was later to be twice
prime minister. Others were practitioners, such as E. F. Schu-
macher, then at the National Coal Board (and subsequently

author of *Small Is Beautiful*). Members of the group themselves also led discussions.

As this approach developed, the earlier limitations placed on attendance became relaxed, with alternates attending at the same time as their principals. The rule governing one firm per industry continued to be strictly enforced, however. In consequence, active membership deepened. It also widened, as the group's reputation spread and new industries were represented. One effect of this widening was to extend the membership to women, at that time very much a minority in business and generally confined to staff functions.

As the meetings increased in size, their venue moved from the Four Feathers to the premises of a respected research institute, Political and Economic Planning. The meetings, however, were no longer the sole activities of the group. The exchange of economic forecasts, which had been one of their features before the pre-dominance of the speaker programme, was developed into the regular preparation of consensus forecasts based on individual forecasts, submitted anonymously. And as membership increased, the first salary surveys were conducted, and proved very popular.

Campbell Fraser stepped down from the chairmanship in June 1957; John Brodrick of the English Electric Company, who had joined the previous year, succeeded him. By now, membership stood at 93, close to three times its original level. This was clearly too many to enable the original social objective to be fulfilled: even the monthly meetings were too large to provide such contact, and were in any case centred increasingly on the external speak-ers. Moreover, as members changed their employers, the original one firm per industry rule had fallen into disuse, the group prefer-ring to retain its members and forgo the confidentiality the rule had been designed to ensure. Meetings therefore came to be regarded as 'off the record', although it was some years before the Chatham House Rule – that proceedings might not be quoted, but information could be noted by those attending for their own use provided the source was not named – was formally adopted.

The Long Term Committee

The group had originally set an upper limit on membership, but this had proved unworkable and had had to be continually raised to accommodate demand and meet the complaints of those who had been placed on the waiting list for membership, even though they met all the necessary criteria. It was clearly necessary to take stock of the group's position and formulate recommendations for its future development: the rules established for the small discussion group envisaged by the founding members were no longer an adequate foundation. A 'Long Term Committee' was therefore established, under the chairmanship of Elwyn Jones, to consider the group's future. It reported, with impressive clarity and brevity, in June 1958. Membership now totalled 127.

The committee's principal conclusion was that 'in view of the continuing demand for membership and the evident need for some association which will provide a meeting ground for the increasing numbers of economists employed in business, the Group should be allowed to go on growing'. Its recommendations were designed to guide and regulate this growth. To this end it identified formally for the first time the purpose of the group:

> ... to serve economists in industry and commerce, or other economists with similar interests. In particular, it should provide a meeting place for business economists where they may exchange views and information and hear expert opinions; and by these means maintain and advance professional standards for business economists and promote their good standing with employers and the public.

Also for the first time, it proposed a guiding definition of business economists:

> ... qualified economists employed in commerce and industry as economists, and economists working elsewhere as economists who have a clear bona fide interest in business economics.

From time to time over the following 45 years, these issues were re-examined, sometimes intensively. Despite this, the original definitions have survived with only minor modifications to render them relevant to changes in the circumstances governing the employment of business economists. The development of the group, and subsequently the Society, has rested on their interpretation rather than changes in their substance.

The Long Term Committee also made a number of practical recommendations. These concerned the extension of membership, including the addition of an 'associate' category; the organisation of activities, notably the creation of small study groups for specific subjects; the size of the management committee, including the desirability of appointing a treasurer; and the name of the group, which it suggested be changed to 'Society of Business Economists'. The recommendations were all accepted, other than that relating to the name. While it was agreed that the name should indeed be changed to reflect better the changed nature of the group, that proposed was felt to be excessively radical and was rejected. In its place, 'Business Economists Group' was adopted. To mark the change, the group decided that it should henceforth use headed notepaper.

Finally, the Long Term Committee recommended that the management committee draft a formal constitution, taking appropriate legal advice. The recommendation was accepted, the demanding task falling primarily to the unfortunate Alan Brazier, as honorary secretary, with the legal advice drawn from Esso. He was also instructed to proceed with the incorporation of the group as a limited liability company. Incorporation as the Business Economists Group duly took place on 12 August 1960. Membership by then stood at approximately 175. That December, the group held its first Christmas party.

Widening: 1958–60

The years between 1958 and 1960 were marked by other changes.

The most immediately relevant to the group's members was probably the launch of an employment service covering both vacancies
and those seeking employment. In terms of the group's professional development, however, the most notable innovation was
without doubt the holding in 1958 of the group's first residential
conference, a small trial event at Pembroke College, Oxford,
organised with the help of a former tutor of Elwyn Jones. This was
most successful, and the following year another, larger and well-
attended conference was held at New College, whereafter it
became an annual fixture. The objective of both the early conferences was to provide members with a refresher course in current
academic economic thinking (rather than theory) of relevance to
business. The conferences lasted four days, including the
weekend. They were to become very popular, clearly fulfilling one
of the basic functions of the group in surroundings that enabled
many of those participating to recall one of the more enjoyable
periods of their lives, while honing their professionalism in the
company of their peers.

At the same time, the first of the separate study groups was
founded. Devoted to the study of the motor industry, it rapidly
led to the problems inherent in all quasi-independent bodies: the
inclusion of non-members who did not meet the membership
requirements of the parent body, and the freedom to comment
publicly without that body's authority. The Motor Industry Suppliers Study Group eventually solved these difficulties by (most
amicably) separating from the parent group and becoming an
independent organisation. Others, later, followed the same
pattern.

Other developments were less positive. Many of the group's
regional members, whose interests had tended to be more market
research oriented than those of the majority in the capital, left the
group en masse (but again with much civility) to join the Industrial Market Research Association. This was disappointing for the
group, but the growth rate in membership was such that it was
easily accommodated. Efforts to launch a journal – the need

which was becoming increasingly apparent – failed, despite lengthy discussions with interested external parties.

Despite such setbacks, 1960 was a significant year for the organisation, which ten years later was to become (somewhat belatedly) the Society of Business Economists. It marked the culmination of a process of organic development, which had begun with a small handful of people seeking mutual support in an austere post-war Britain, ending with a recognised body of similar professionals in a recognisably modern economy showing the first signs of an emerging affluence. The structure then established has persisted to the present, despite major changes in the economic, social and political environment. In 1960, it provided an essential foundation for the group's next phase of development. This was to last twenty years, and see the group treble in size, expanding its activities, and its influence, accordingly.

The rise to maturity: 1960–80

From group to society

Although 1960 was a significant year in the group's history, it did not mark any discontinuity in its development. The following three years witnessed three chairmen, but this was the result of Charles Sharpston, who had succeeded John Brodrick at the end of 1960, being transferred by his employer to Brazil. He was replaced by the honorary secretary, Alan Brazier, for a period of two years, at which point Tad Rybczynski was elected chairman and both Brazier and the replacement honorary secretary, Colin Robinson, resigned from the committee (possibly with relief). In the meantime the group continued to grow in both membership and activities. In 1962, the papers from the annual conference – tablished event – were published for the first time under *nning*. They cost six shillings (£0.30). The conferences however, were not profitable, and the Christmas party eable loss as a result of a failure of many attendees to this, the group's finances remained broadly in balance, helped by occasional and mild subscription increases.

Administration, in contrast, remained an increasing problem. With the group now much too large and complex to be administered from the honorary secretary's office, an outside secretariat was essential. However, the arrangement with PEP was becoming unsustainably expensive. The service was moved to the Economic Research Council, but this was a failure, and a further move was made in 1962 to the Society of Investment Analysts. This proved a significant improvement, possibly because of the similarity in the administrative demands of the two bodies, although the group remained de facto the junior partner.

In the same year, the group was approached by a recently created parallel organisation of new economics graduates working in industry, with a view to collaboration. Constructive discussion ensued, and led to the absorption of the new body into the group as a graduates section. To cater for the particular needs of its members, this had its own programme and a lower subscription. Its members, however, could participate in the group's activities, and the group's members were encouraged to attend the graduate section's meetings. The innovation proved extremely successful, but over time had the unintended consequence of segregating the younger members from their older peers, leading to a sense of exclusion for the former. The section was eventually disbanded in 1968, by which time it had over 80 members, and its membership integrated into the group as a whole.

When Brazier and Robinson stepped down at the end of 1963, membership stood at some 370, over ten times the number who had been identified at the first founding meeting ten years earlier. Over that time, the group had been developed by an unusually talented group of people, whose ability to combine their efforts towards the achievement of a common goal had been honed in the experiences of wartime and austerity. The style of management had been essentially collegiate, as befitted a society; although the efforts of some had had more long-term influence than others, all involved had contributed in an active and cohesive fashion.

Since first joining the group in 1958, Tad Rybczynski, the incoming chairman in 1963, had been among these enthusiastic participants. A former RAF bomber pilot (as were other early members) and a formidable intellect, he had the unusual distinction of having given his name to a theorem which had subsequently become part of the standard theory of the economics of international trade. In consequence he had an international academic reputation. He also had a profound belief in the ability of business economics to bridge the widening gulf between academic theory and business practice, to the benefit not only of individual enterprises but of the management of finance and the economy as a whole. He therefore felt that the group had a mission beyond that of its constitution. To fulfil this it had to both continue to grow and achieve a stature commensurate with that aim. And it had to do so with the full support and participation of its members.

Much of the foundation needed for this ambition already existed as a result of the work of the previous ten years, but not all. One of Rybczynski's early acts was to propose an amendment to the constitution to provide for the election of a president and up to five vice-presidents, to provide the group with connections it might not otherwise be able to command, and give assistance in other ways as necessary. The proposal was approved at an extraordinary general meeting on 15 September 1964. The first president, Sir Robert Shone, director-general of the National Economic Development Office, was elected the following year, although it was to be some further time before he was to be joined by any vice-presidents, those initially invited having declined.

The annual conference that year attracted 140 participants and discussed the theme of 'Business Strategy and Economic Growth'; its programme was slightly less academically oriented than had hitherto been the norm. A survey of the business economists' function was launched with assistance from Strathclyde University, with a view to the publication of a book based on the results. The Short Term Forecasting Group, led by James Morrell, began to publish its results quarterly in *The Times*. A new one-day economic outlook conference was launched. It attracted 160 attendees, including economic journalists, and received good press coverage. The group's university liaison efforts were strengthened, with a more precise objective: to help members communicate with academic specialists and so develop a two-way relationship between the group and relevant academics. The monthly meetings were moved from Locomotive House to the more distinguished Chatham House. And work resumed on the possible publication of a journal.

To achieve this level of activity required resources, in the shape of additional committee members to shoulder some of the burdens. The constitutional rule that limited the size of the committee to twelve was therefore conveniently overlooked. The committee rose first to fourteen, then to sixteen. All were active. With few resignations, and those mainly for personal reasons, continuity did not present a problem. The administration of the group, however, was less smooth. In 1966, the Society of Investment Analysts terminated its agreement. The secretarial service was transferred to a lobbying organisation, Britain in Europe (the UK was not at that time a member of the European Economic Community). This was not a success, and a year later it was moved again, to Freelance Work for Women, a centrally organised network of women working from home. The group's work was allocated to a young mother living in South London, named Marian Marshall. The change was beneficial, but after two years the agency reallocated the assignment following the Marshall family's relocation to Watford. The result was unsatisfactory, and in 1970 the arrangement with the agency was terminated, and the relationship with Marian re-established on a direct basis. It was the beginning of a lasting partnership, which created and maintained the permanent support the group needed, enabling it to be managed in a professional way. Marian was given full secretarial authority in 1973, and was appointed executive secretary, the post she still holds, three years later.

The second half of the 1960s were spent developing the group in the directions now established. In the area of university liaison, six universities were targeted, and a programme of quarterly seminars set up to bring members and academics therefrom together. Further sub-groups were formed to cover industrial long-term planning and manpower – the latter later separating to become the prestigious Manpower Society. There were now eight such groups, the others embracing statistics; the 'overseas economy'; short-term forecasting; corporate planning; the City; and interest rates. Relationships with other bodies – notably the Royal Economic Society and the Organisation of Professional Users of Statistics – were strengthened, and provincial activity reinforced through an association with the Manchester Statistical Society.

Active contact was also made with business economists' organisations overseas. In Europe, the group participated in expanding the Council of European Economists, a loose contact group of national associations, and made early approaches of a deeper nature to the newly formed French association, AFEDE. In the United States, fruitful exchanges took place with the National Association of Business Economists (NABE), which led to NABE members attending the annual conference in Cambridge in 1969, and some 60 group members attending the 1970 NABE annual conference in Boston as guests. Three years later, the three associations jointly launched the International Federation of Associations of Business Economists (IFABE) at a major conference in Paris.

And perhaps most significantly, the journal, *The Business Economist*, was at last launched, with Rybczynski himself as editor, helped by George Ray and Ulric Spencer.

Not all the progress was smooth, however. In 1968, the annual conference returned a loss, despite an excellent programme. (Ironically, its subject had been 'Inflation'.) Attendance at the one-day economic outlook conference settled at a level below that of the early figures, and press comment became more muted. There was some feeling that the name of the group was now a hindrance to its ambitions. A survey of members' opinions in 1968 had revealed insufficient support to warrant a change; the following year that support had become an overwhelming majority. The name 'Society of Business Economists' was formally adopted shortly thereafter.

The making of a profession

To confirm that its policies were in line with members' interests, in 1970 the Society set up a working party to examine its own future. Membership was drawn carefully to balance experience, employment and age. The 'Special Committee on Future Policy and Progress of the Society' met eleven times and conducted an extensive survey of members' attitudes. Its report ran to 35 pages of single spacing. (The version circulated to members was abbreviated!) Its conclusions endorsed the direction now being taken, and it emphasised the need to establish a professional status for the business economist, possibly with appropriate examinations, without ignoring the other aspects of the Society's objectives, particularly the desire of members to have social contact. It also confirmed the need for a permanent secretariat. Finally, it identified a high level of acceptability for higher subscriptions among members. This was of no small importance: the Society's growth in activities ahead of commensurate growth in income (even though membership now stood at around 580) had led to a deteriorating financial position.

As the 1970s progressed, the policies endorsed by the Special Committee began to bear fruit. The Society was invited to submit its members' views to government on the effects on business of membership of the EEC; and to the Sandilands Committee on inflation accounting. It also helped to organise a top-level conference on EEC entry at Sussex University. The monthly meetings were being addressed regularly by speakers of political and economic significance. (These had included Sir Keith Joseph, a principal architect of Margaret Thatcher's policies. The attendance at that meeting remains a record.) At one such meeting, Sir Ronald McIntosh, the director-general of the National Economic

Development Office, announced a new national economic planning exercise based heavily on business participation. The 1975 annual conference, at King's College, Cambridge, provided the forum for a series of top-level exchanges between industry and government on the need (or otherwise) for a more proactive industrial policy. The previous year, the annual dinner had celebrated the 21st anniversary of the founding of the Society, and had been attended by five former heads of the Government Economic Service, including Lord Roberthall, who had succeeded Sir Richard Stone as president between 1968 and 1973. The dinner had been chaired by the Society's new president, Campbell Fraser.

This progress had not been achieved without controversy. Despite the inflationary environment – particularly after the oil crisis of 1973 – and the findings of the Special Committee, subscription increases aroused strong opposition, and the Council (which by now had returned to its statutory size of twelve) was felt by some to be remote from the real interests of the members. This was a misconception, but indicative of the stresses associated with the drive for development. One effect of this controversy was to attract members of unusually high calibre to serve on the Council. Efforts were made to link the work of Council members with the wider membership, but these took time to mature. In the meantime, discussion at Council meetings was not always peaceful, although the outcome was invariably constructive.

Rybczynski stepped down from the chairmanship in 1975. He felt by then that he had achieved most of what he had set out to do. The Society and the profession were well established in circles of influence and power, although it would be some years yet before the position of chief economist would command the status and salary of its potential. Membership had reached 656; the task now was to open up the Society further without losing the professional depth that business economists had achieved.

The incoming chairman, Peter Gordon-Potts, set out to achieve that objective, and over the next three and a half years did so. The level of activity, and the extent to which members were involved therein, rose markedly. The status that Rybczynski had conferred on the Society was now used to consolidate the Society's position. An early example of this occurred with the second IFABE conference, which was held at King's College, Cambridge, in 1976. Attended by some 300 members of the three societies, together with guests from other countries, and imaginatively organised by Douglas Drage, its speakers included Henry Wallich, a governor of the Federal Reserve, and John Kenneth Galbraith. The latter's after-dinner address was chaired with considerable skill by the member of the Council who had (*inter alia*) been involved deeply in establishing the first IFABE conference, Detta (now Baroness) o'Cathain. International relations continued to be a theme of the Society, particularly within Europe. Three years later Gordon-Potts was instrumental in establishing a European equivalent of IFABE, EuroFABE, becoming its first chairman.

Other activities continued to expand. A major debate was conducted on the subject of the government's proposed 'planning agreements' with large companies. A programme of seminars – known as the Falush seminars, after their founder – was introduced, covering issues such as exchange rates, profit trends, inflation accounting, and devaluation versus import controls, subjects of mounting concern as inflation remained high and the performance of the economy weak. The 1977 King's College conference was entitled 'The Re-industrialisation of Britain', a theme that now looks eccentric but was then of growing concern. It was well attended, and the proceedings were published (as indeed had been those of some previous conferences). Management of the journal, which had been facing such problems of poor circulation that the publisher withdrew, was placed on a new footing with a managing editor (Robert Jones), editor (David Kingston) and review editor (as before, Ulric Spencer). Production was brought in-house. A book on careers for business economists was produced, to cater for an increasing demand for guidance from universities.

Despite the standing of the Society, it had in the past proved difficult to fill the positions of vice-president accommodated by the constitution, and the vacancies had been left in abeyance. A new effort was made in 1977, this time successfully, and Sir John Partridge, KBE, became the first vice-president. He was succeeded over the following two years by Sir Donald MacDougall and Lord Armstrong of Sanderstead. In 1978, to commemorate the 25th anniversary of the Society's founding, the annual dinner included as guests as many of the founding members as were able to come. In the event, eight attended, in addition to the president and the first president, Sir Robert Shone, and the vice-presidents.

Not all progress was smooth – among other problems Gordon-Potts became the first chairman to face the prospect of legal action from a highly influential institution as a result of a forthcoming journal article by a rival body. But despite the growing discord in the national economy, by 1979 the Society had clearly reached a vibrant maturity, and a balance of activities that was, in Gordon-Potts's own words, 'just about right'. Horizontal expansion was now likely to incur diseconomies of scale and be counter-productive.

Inflation, recession and survival: 1980–5

The Callaghan government fell in May 1979, and was replaced by that of Margaret Thatcher. With it the economic philosophies that had formed the background to the whole of the Society's life were rapidly eclipsed. Inflation was already high; attempts to control it through income restraint and price controls having failed, they were abandoned and interest rates raised to historically high levels. The exchange rate followed suit. Manufacturing industry, which accounted for some two-thirds of the Society's membership, was plunged into deep recession.

The Society's financial health was vulnerable, as was that of all such institutions, to volume. A relatively small fall-off in revenue resulted rapidly in a loss. If left unattended, the loss would escalate. This problem had haunted the Society since its foundation; high inflation exacerbated it substantially. Conscious of the need to provide for such difficulties, the Society had built up

investments throughout the 1970s, largely through the astute management of the able treasurer, Don Fair, but these had other priorities. In 1980, the Council, now with Rufus Godson in the chair,
faced such a problem. It decided it had no option but to raise subscriptions by 50 per cent. Some membership would be lost, but the
increase would more than compensate, and the position would
return to balance. The increase took effect in 1982. Membership
was then some 720, slightly off its peak of 734, reached in 1979.
A working party set up to examine the Society's finances reported
shortly afterwards. Its findings were accepted, but its recommendations rejected. The Council set up a consultants' register to help
those who might be losing their jobs as a result of the recession. It
proved very valuable and grew rapidly.

The recession proved to be very deep. Over the following two
years, some 40 per cent of the members were made redundant.
Their adherence to the Society proved to be strong, but membership still fell by some 15 per cent. The casualties were virtually all
in manufacturing. Many became independent consultants, some
joined the financial sector. Working hours increased markedly,
leaving less time and energy for outside professional activity.
Weekend events became unpopular. It was clear that the Society
had to be reshaped to meet the needs of this new world, and that a
way had to be found to return its finances to long-term balance.

Rufus Godson had resigned as chairman in 1982, to be
replaced by Donald Anderson. Both Godson and Gordon-Potts
remained on the Council, but Don Fair, after many years of distinguished and graceful service as treasurer, retired. The Council,
with Robert Jones now in the difficult position of treasurer, set
about examining every aspect of the Society's activities and
testing them against members' opinions. It was an intense and
lengthy task, conducted with the intention of preserving as much
as was feasible of the Society's activities, while defending, at all
costs, the Society's excellent reputation. In the event, it was successful, the only identifiable casualty being the annual conference,
which was no longer felt to be viable. Cost-saving measures were

taken in a number of areas. These included the journal, whose frequency was reduced on a temporary basis to two issues a year, and the monthly meetings. The latter moved from the RAC Club, where they had held been since Chatham House had become unavailable some years earlier, to Unilever House – a venue not only cheaper but also more agreeable. The changes were balanced by a slimming down of the administration, a very difficult and at times painful task in the close culture of the Society. Its achievement without disruption said much for the cohesion of the Society as an institution, and for the dedication and goodwill of the secretariat, who had to bear the brunt of the process.

Membership stabilised in 1985, at around 605. Sir Campbell Fraser (who had been knighted in 1978) retired from the presidency and was succeeded by Sir Adrian Cadbury; Gordon-Potts left the Council after eleven years' service. Sir Terence Burns became a vice-president, filling a vacancy left by Sir John Partridge. With Lord Roll of Ipsden having succeeded Sir Robert Armstrong in 1981, all three vice-presidents were now current or former Treasury knights.

By 1985 the financial situation was decidedly healthier. In the interim, the Society had been involved in two notable events, both in the international arena. The first of these was the third Euro-FABE conference, held in Rome in 1984. The timing of this conference was particularly apt, coming at the start of the development of the Single Market, and it was devoted to an interactive examination of the European economy and its structure. Among those attending was Romano Prodi, now president of the European Commission. EuroFABE held several subsequent conferences, but never again achieved the same degree of relevance. The second was the fifth IFABE conference, held in London in 1985. Again, the theme – international trade – proved exceptionally timely, as the Uruguay Round of trade negotiations was about to begin. Despite significant problems with the programme, which resulted in the formation of lasting friendships with members of NABE, the conference was impeccably organised by the secretariat and was an outstanding success. It included a memorable dinner, held in the Banqueting House in Whitehall, which particularly impressed those from abroad. It would be, as the NABE representative who was to be responsible for a future IFABE conference in Washington commented as he surveyed the surroundings, 'a hard act to follow'.

Anderson stepped down as chairman that November, and was succeeded by David Kingston, a former editor of the journal. Jones retired from the Council after fourteen years' service; Anderson and Godson stayed on to give the customary continuity. It had been a very difficult three years: to add to its structural problems, the Society was beginning to suffer from demographic effects as more established members reached retirement than new members joined. In addition, the Society had been subject throughout the recession to attempts at infiltration by political groups and others with the intention of using it as a mouthpiece for their own ends. But despite radical changes in the employment patterns of its membership, it had more than survived, and had retained its integrity.

The road to distinction: 1986–2003

By mid-1986, membership stood at 606, more than 17 per cent below its 1979 peak. Over the following fifteen years, it returned to slow growth, although it was never to reach the heights achieved in 1979, and even in 2002 remained at only 87 per cent of that level. The majority of members were now employed in finance, many of the rest in consulting. Most industrial departments had been closed or their functions taken over by other areas, such as business development. And the function of the business economist had changed markedly, in some cases fundamentally. These changes were not confined to the UK. They were examined in depth in a series of articles in both *Business Economics*, the NABE journal, and *The Business Economist* throughout 1986.

'Big Bang', the ending of single capacity in the City and the subsequent rapid growth of the financial sector, greatly enhanced both the importance and the incomes of business economists, and was beneficial to the Society. As international competition inten- sified, and globalisation developed, the consulting sector also grew substantially, and with it the role of the business economist. At the same time, working hours became much extended, and overseas travel became common at all career levels.

The Society had to adjust accordingly. The emphasis again moved towards professional competence, and the social aspects gave way to professional networking. These changes happened gradually. Among the earliest was the creation in 1987 of two new categories of member: fellows and students. The introduction of the former was slightly controversial, and was agreed only after strict limitations had been placed on both the criteria required and the proportion of the total membership who would be permitted to enjoy this new status, and the higher subscription that it demanded. Both innovations undoubtedly enhanced the Society. In retrospect they can be seen as an early recognition of the direc- tion in which it now had to travel.

By 1989, as Kingston handed over the chair to Jim Hirst (but remained, as was customary, on the Council), the journal had returned to its former three issues per year, and was becoming in some ways the key instrument of the Society. Other activities, however, were still well supported and had changed little. Now, as the structure of the financial community developed and the exter- nal environment remained volatile, they too had to be restructured. The most obvious changes occurred in two areas. The first of these was that of the one-day conference on the economic outlook, which was reduced to a half-day, plus lunch, and its subject matter broadened to embrace matters of current concern. To ensure its continued appeal, an outside guest figure was introduced to chair the proceedings as a comprehensive whole. The new formula was an immediate success, and remains in place. The incidence of more focused activities such as special conferences and seminars, and study groups, was also increased. Notable among these was the Structural Change group, founded by Susan Bluff (who tragically died a few years later), which attracted considerable attention in view of the pertinence of its subject matter.

The second area of change concerned international liaison, the attraction of which to the membership declined markedly as their own international travel increased. The first manifestation of this occurred in 1990 when, after a considerable amount of work by Society members, and notably Richard Freeman, to create a viable event, the Barcelona EuroFABE conference had to be cancelled. There were other factors involved in the cancellation, themselves a manifestation of cultural differences within the EU, but the trend was evident. Efforts were made to develop substitute activities, such as joint forecasts, but these failed to gain momentum. In 1991 the Society, whose contribution to EuroFABE was the largest amongst the organisation's member associations, decided that it could no longer justify using its resources in this way, and withdrew from membership. This pragmatic, essentially Anglo-Saxon decision was received with considerable hostility by some other member associations at the time, and it was a little while before relationships returned to normal. The Society's participation in IFABE was similarly slimmed down, although it remains a member and continues to participate in the biannual conferences.

Perhaps the most significant changes, however, were to the journal, which was upgraded to enable it better to fulfil its developing function of a major tool of the Society, and relaunched. Issues continued to be themed, but new features were added, notably 'Speakers' Corner', which gave detailed reports of the addresses at the monthly meetings, and the inclusion of comments and criticisms of articles. Its compact size was retained, but its publication, which had been handled in-house, was transferred to an outside company. Reaction to the changes was very positive. The editorial work involved had now become considerable, and it was decided that the editor – now Hirst, who had handed over the chairmanship to Andrew Sentence in 1995 – should be supported by an editorial board.

Other innovations have been less profound, but important nevertheless. Since the mid-1990s, the Society has had an interactive Internet site, a marketing manager for the journal, and a press officer. It organises professional workshops and holds annual meetings with senior members of the Treasury and the Bank of England. Its annual dinner has become a central event, held in noble surroundings, and is addressed by some of the most influential members of the global economic scene. The 2002 dinner was attended by some 220 members and guests – the number of the latter the largest on record. And in recent years the dinner has also been the occasion for the presentation of the annual Rybczynski Prize, first awarded in 2001 in memory of Tad Rybczynski, who died in 1999. The prize is given to the author submitting the best piece of writing in business economics, published or unpublished, as judged by a panel. It attracts a high quality of entry.

Reflections

The Society is now 50 years old. In retrospect, its development has benefited greatly from the continuity of its governing bodies and its secretariat. Despite the demanding responsibilities incurred, and the priorities of their own careers, the Council has been marked by the willingness of its members to serve for long periods: the longest-serving current member, Rosemary Connell, is in her 24th year. (And, although not a Council member, Ulric Spencer is in his 32nd year as the journal's reviews editor.) The dedication of others, few of whom it has been possible to name in this short history, has been similarly remarkable. Most have extended their contributions well beyond any single responsibility. And the close identification of the secretariat with the Society's members and aims has been a keystone since 1967.

In addition to the seamlessness of the Council, currently chaired by John Calverley, the Society has been very well served by its presidents. In recent years these have included Sir Denys Henderson, who had succeeded Sir Adrian Cadbury in 1990, Sir

David Lees and Lord Burns of Pitshanger. As a former vice-president and speaker at the Society's meetings and conferences of many years' standing, Terry Burns is as familiar to many of the current membership as Sir Campbell Fraser had been to the founding generation.

He presides over a Society with a remarkably loyal membership, but one that has perhaps only in the last few years achieved the ambitions set by earlier generations. That it has now done so has been exemplified recently in two ways. First, two of its members, both from business, are currently independent members of the Bank of England's Monetary Policy Committee. This is not the Society's only connection with that committee: two recently elected vice-presidents, Sir Alan Budd (previously a fellow) and DeAnne Julius, have both been members thereof. But it is the first time the Society has had active members in positions of this kind at the centre of UK economic management, a situation that would have been unthinkable over much of its life.

The second, although somewhat different in kind, is equally telling. The Society recently held a rather unusual meeting, again at the Bank of England. It was fully booked, and there was a waiting list to attend. There were three people on the podium: the governor of the Bank of England, Sir Edward George, as host; the chairman of the board of governors of the Federal Reserve System, Alan Greenspan, as speaker; and the Society's chairman, as chairman. The Society had clearly come a long way from the Four Feathers.

Note

1   Former Director of Communications and Economics at the Courtaulds Group, and a former chairman of the Society of Business Economists.

INDEX

employment 35; GDP 28; labour
market 22, 23–4, 33–5; part-time
24; productivity growth 25
enterprise culture 75
environment 29, 61, 63; auditors
64; damage 29, 31; economics of
163; Kyoto accords 151;
productivity 36; responsibility vs
profitability 54–65; strategic
planning 160
equivalence theorem 177, 178
Ericsson, N. R. 147
euro 80, 130, 131, 135, 138, 148, 157
EuroFABE 195, 198, 201
European Central Bank (ECB) 106,
107
European Economic Community
(EEC) 13, 69, 157, 193
European Exchange Rate
Mechanism (ERM) 48, 76–8,
80–1, 133–5; monetary
tightening 103; Stability and
Growth Pact 92, 106, 107; UK
withdrawal 87, 106, 135, 149
European Monetary System (EMS)
76, 134
European Monetary Union (EMU)
14, 106–7, 126–7, 136–7, 157
European sclerosis 157
European Social Model 80
European Union 12, 13, 69, 121;
CSR Green Paper 56;
sustainability reporting 56;
temporary workers 79
evolutionary approach 175–6
exchange markets, foreign 163
exchange rates, 1990s rise 148;
deflation 52; fixed 14, 43–4;
floating 15, 44, 72, 74, 78, 92,
132–3; sterling overvaluation
138; targeting 131, 134–5; USA
72

expansionary policies 15, 21
exports, world 12
external shocks 160–1

Fair, Don 197
Falush seminars 195
Family Expenditure Survey 32
firm, theory of 163, 167, 174–6
first-mover advantage 59, 63
floating exchange rates 15, 44, 72,
74, 78, 92, 132–3
flows, balance of payments 128–9,
130; capital 12, 17
flying pickets 71
forecasting 6–7, 32–6, 153;
econometric models 143–4, 145,
154, 155; error sources 146–9;
foreign exchange 127; future of
141–52; inflation 49–53;
macroeconomic 166
foreign exchange trading 12
France 47–8; GDP 27–8; growth
35
Fraser, Sir Campbell 182, 183, 184,
194, 198
free competition 83
free markets 70, 83
free trade 9, 12
Freelance Work for Women 191
Freeman, Richard 3, 6, 153–65,
201
Friedman, Milton 84, 114, 133
Friedmanites 76
FTSE⁴Good Index 57

Gaitskell, Hugh 104–5
Galbraith, John Kenneth 195
game theory 163, 166
GDP, Asian crisis 150; forecasting
33, 34–7; government
expenditure 116–17;
international comparisons 26–8;